"This book is an essential, evidence-based guide for helping teens and young adults build the real-world skills needed for confident independence. Drawing on years of clinical experience, the authors offer practical tools, clear frameworks, and engaging exercises that address everything from decision-making and distress tolerance to family dynamics and financial realities. This book stands out for its proactive, skills-focused approach, making it invaluable for young adults, parents, and professionals alike. A timely, empowering road-map for thriving in adulthood rather than merely getting by."

David Tolin, *Ph.D., Director of the Institute of Living/Anxiety Disorders Center*

"Drs. Kaplan, Villavicencio, and Dumessa have provided an invaluable resource that addresses the critically important topic of young adults struggling to develop the skills needed to thrive without high levels of parental support. It provides specific, practical guidance and information on the steps parents and young adults can take to make meaningful, lasting change. It is highly recommended!"

Jonathan Dalton, *Ph.D., Director of the Center for Anxiety and Behavioral Change, Rockville MD*

Launching into Young Adulthood

The transition from adolescence to adulthood can be challenging. This easy-to-read guide on "how to succeed" as a young adult provides hands-on tools for building emotional awareness and psychological skills to successfully navigate early adulthood.

Written by experts in clinical psychology, this transformational book provides a contextual background and a specific, proactive plan to prepare young adults to become independent from their primary caregivers as they enter adulthood. Detailed yet accessible, this book explores essential topics from a psychological perspective, including decision-making, goal-setting, identifying strengths and weaknesses, managing distress and "successful failures," understanding social connections and expectations, and how to use your unique skills to your advantage. Real-life examples are presented to illustrate how to work through potential problems young adults face when entering independent life, with additional activities, exercises, and questionnaires to aid in learning and development.

This book is an ideal resource for young adults looking to equip themselves with the skills to tackle the transition into adulthood. It is also a helpful guide for parents and caregivers, as well as mental health professionals who work with adolescents, teens, and young adults.

Johanna Kaplan, Ph.D., is a licensed clinical psychologist and director of the Washington Anxiety Center of Capitol Hill (WACCH) in Washington, DC.

Anna Villavicencio, Ph.D., is a clinical psychologist at the Washington Anxiety Center of Capitol Hill (WACCH). She is an adjunct lecturer in the Department of Psychology at Catholic University of America, where she teaches classes in psychological disorders and adult psychopathology.

Lediya Dumessa, Ph.D., is a clinical psychologist at Washington Anxiety Center of Capitol Hill (WACCH). She is a graduate research assistant in Resilience and Regulation Lab at Mississippi State University.

Launching into Young Adulthood

Evidence-Based Tools and Psychological Skills to Help Teens Succeed

Johanna Kaplan, Anna Villavicencio and Lediya Dumessa

Routledge
Taylor & Francis Group
NEW YORK AND LONDON

Designed cover image: Getty Images

First published 2027
by Routledge
605 Third Avenue, New York, NY 10158

and by Routledge
4 Park Square, Milton Park, Abingdon, Oxon, OX14 4RN

Routledge is an imprint of the Taylor & Francis Group, an informa business

ISBN: 9781041093053 (hbk)
ISBN: 9781041093046 (pbk)
ISBN: 9781003649410 (ebk)

DOI: 10.4324/9781003649410

Typeset in Optima
by codeMantra

Contents

Acknowledgments

This book has been a true labor of love over the past 15 years. It would not have been possible without the support of my amazing husband, Tim, and my two everything, Ellie and Tucker. Nancy Kaplan taught me the skills to succeed as an adult, and I owe her everything. I also owe thanks to Dr. Dumessa and Dr. Villavicencio for their friendship, collaboration, and invaluable insight in this venture.

Dr. Johanna Kaplan

This work would not have been possible without the dedication and expertise of my coauthors, Dr. Kaplan and Dr. Dumessa. I greatly appreciate their collaboration and encouragement throughout this project. I am also deeply grateful to my husband for his support, and to my teen son, whose journey toward young adulthood was the inspiration behind my contributions to this book. Finally, my efforts here are offered in loving memory of my father, Marco, whose lessons in life skills shaped the person and clinician I am today. He is with me in this work always.

Dr. Anna Villavicencio

I am deeply grateful to my coauthors, Dr. Kaplan and Dr. Villavicencio, whose expertise and dedication enriched this book and my understanding of the young adults and families we serve. To my husband, Ruf, thank you for believing in me and encouraging me to pursue work that matters deeply to me. To my daughters, Amnen and Malden, you are my greatest joy and my daily reminder that growth is rarely linear and always worthy of patience and wonder. To my parents, Aynua and Babsho, I owe so much of who I am today to your sacrifices, courage, and the opportunities you created for us. To my brothers, Miky and Naty, thank you for always being in my corner.

Dr. Lediya Dumessa

We are indebted to our colleagues at the Washington Anxiety Center of Capitol Hill, the middle and high schools we frequently consult with, and the patients we have treated with *failure to launch*. Without their contributions, the Life-Prep Program—designed to prevent this persistent and challenging condition—would not have been possible to develop.

1 Defining the Problem

What Is the Common Saying, "Failure to Launch" and What Does It Mean to Be a Successful, Independent Young Adult?

"Failure to Launch" is a phrase that is commonly used to describe the inability of young adults to develop sufficient life skills that facilitate transition into independent adulthood as well as cope with more complicated, environmental stressors. This may involve the inability to obtain and maintain employment or pursue higher education, live independently, gain financial stability, maintain stable relationships, pursue personal hobbies and goals, and have less overall reliance on their original parents/caretakers. As of 2022, half of young adults in the United States between the ages of 18 and 29 were still living with their parents.[1] In a retirement investment survey in 2023, almost 60% of 18–42-year-olds were found to still depend financially on the support of their caretakers.[2]

Although becoming a successful, independent adult can vary by person and is impacted by cultural and societal factors, there are common milestones and markers we often associate with the transition to adulthood. For example, beginning in late adolescence (around 18 years), young adults begin making decisions about their future regarding higher education, vocational training, or joining the workforce upon graduating high school. As such, in their early twenties, some pursue further education and career opportunities while others may start working full-time or part-time to gain work experience and financial independence. By their mid-twenties, many young adults complete their college or vocational education (unless pursuing further education) and start careers or establish stability in their employment. During this period, they often claim and seek out more independence, as they move out of their parent/caretakers' home and take on more responsibility related to finances and household management. Their late twenties and early thirties can be a period when young adults further establish stability and independence as they advance in their careers, get married, or start families. While it is important to remember that the transition to adulthood does not look the same both in nature and timeline, there is a general expectation for young adults to assume increased independence and stability over time. It is when this gradual progression does

DOI: 10.4324/9781003649410-1

not initiate, gets interrupted, or is sidelined that parents or guardians often become concerned about a young adult's independent future. Let us look at the following case example.

"Josh"

"Josh" is a 22-year-old self-identified man who recently graduated from a 4-year college. He lives with his parents in a suburban neighborhood. Despite his age, Josh has not been able to gain employment or pursue an advanced degree, which has led to significant challenges in his quest for independence. Although Josh has applied for numerous jobs, he has faced difficulty in securing stable employment. His lack of work experience and limited networking opportunities have made job hunting a frustrating experience. Josh's financial situation is a source of stress. He relies on his parents for financial support, including housing, groceries, and other necessities. The longer Josh waits to pursue opportunities, the harder the opportunities are to find, and result in a cycle of lack of momentum, discouragement, and overall reliance on his caretakers. Financial dependency on his parents has strained his relationship with them and diminished his sense of autonomy. The combination of unemployment and uncertainty about his future has taken a toll on Josh's emotional well-being. He experiences episodes of anxiety and self-doubt, which further hinder his ability to take decisive steps toward independence. Josh's limited experience with independent living has left him lacking in essential life skills, such as budgeting, cooking, and household management. He feels ill-prepared to take on the responsibilities of living on his own.

It is no surprise that lack of gaining functional independence as a young adult can have dire consequences for the individual as well as society at large. A young adult's inability to join the workforce and become financially independent, for example, can quickly strain family resources as they rely on parents for support. The prolonged dependence on parents can also negatively impact parental well-being and strain family relationships as parents experience increased financial and emotional stress. The lack of direction in life coupled with social stigma surrounding *failure to launch* can then lead to a young adult experiencing low self-esteem, feelings of inadequacy, as well as mental health issues such as anxiety and depression.

The underlying causes of *failure to launch* can vary and may include factors such as psychological or emotional issues, a lack of motivation or direction, financial dependence, or a fear of failure and the accompanying responsibilities. In the chapters to come, we will discuss identifying and building the skills and knowledge that could help *increase* your or your child's chances of becoming a *successful*, independent young adult.

It is very important to underline that we do not assign a value judgment to what it means to be a successfully launched adult. As discussed above, this definition is wide and varied. However, we do know that individuals without a self-defined purpose, goals, and lack of autonomy in their life (whether related to housing, finances, etc.) do have a higher risk of anxiety and depression.[3,4] Therefore, an individual can launch on their own terms, but within the parameters of achieving and even mastering the skills discussed in this book. This plan allows for an individual to sustain life satisfaction and productivity as life naturally ebbs and flows.

The Role of Underlying Mental Health Conditions

Underlying mental health conditions such as anxiety and its related disorders (social anxiety, obsessive compulsive disorder, panic disorder), depression, learning disorders, executive functioning disorders (e.g., attention deficit/hyperactivity disorder, ADHD), and developmental disorders can significantly compromise an individual's ability to manage independent living by decreasing motivation and self-efficacy (i.e., the ability we have to know that we can succeed and have the internal and external skills to succeed no matter what we face in life). Notably, a significant portion (about 40%) of young adults who have not gained successful independence have symptoms of and/or meet criteria for a clinical anxiety and/or depressive disorder.[5] However, approximately 60% of these young adults who have not launched successfully do not necessarily have a clinical disorder but are just lacking in the essential skills and experience to become a successful and independent young adult. In terms of clinical disorders, specific anxiety disorders such as social anxiety disorder can have a direct contribution to *failure to launch,* as they can lead to avoidance of school or workplace environments, fear of evaluation by others, performance-related fears, poor tolerance in uncertain social situations, and fear of authority figures such as teachers and employers. Another anxiety disorder, panic disorder, can lead to association of panic symptoms with the workplace environment, lack of self-efficacy, avoidance of environments that feel "unsafe," and fear of uncertainty, in general. Similarly, depression is characterized by lack of energy, motivation, concentration, and interests which are all needed to pursue independent goals in life. If a young adult is experiencing depression, they may not be able to wake up on time in the morning and have the energy to drive to work and be functional at a job.

Relatedly, skills deficits in the areas of executive functioning, emotion regulation, and coping are also significant contributors to *failure to launch*. Executive functioning, which refers to cognitive processes that help us plan, organize, initiate, and manage time effectively, impacts our ability to set and achieve goals, maintain routines, and be self-directed—in other words—skills necessary for independent living. Lack of emotion regulation skills can lead to impulsive decision-making, which can have negative consequences further impacting independence. For example, if someone cannot tolerate getting negative feedback in the workplace, they may continually quit their job in search of one that always (not necessarily realistic) provides them positive feedback. Similarly, lack of coping skills or the use of unhelpful coping strategies such as avoidance can have negative consequences. Avoidance, which often stems from the fear of facing challenges, can lead to lack of progress in personal development. It is not just a job or finding an apartment that can stem from avoidance behaviors but even the smaller behaviors of learning how to look for a job, how to edit a resume, and how to reach out and call employers. Avoidance of smaller, more productive behaviors can lead to avoidance of the activities needed to gain successful independence.

Another contributing factor to failure to launch is the ever-changing definition of adolescence. In the 1980s–1990s, adolescence was seen as a relatively brief developmental stage; its definition has now expanded to include a larger span of life. In recent decades, there has been a growing recognition of "extended adolescence." This refers to the idea that many young people are taking longer to achieve traditional markers of adulthood, such as financial independence and starting a family. This trend is influenced by factors like higher education, economic pressures, and changing social norms. During the Obama presidential administration, healthcare privileges were extended to "children" aged 26 years and below under their caretakers/parents. Prior to this, one motivation for young adults gaining independence was having to gain healthcare coverage on their own, an important impetus for gaining successful employment (where the employment package would include healthcare, retirement, etc.).

Relevant Research Related to Generation Z and Millennials

There is generally limited research on not becoming successful, independent young adults as a whole; however, there are relevant generational characteristics that are related to the phenomenon and upcoming cultural crisis. Generation Z (Gen Z) includes individuals born between 1997 and 2012. According to the American Psychological Association, Gen Z young adults (18–24) are more likely to report poor mental health conditions, including anxiety and depression, as compared to previous generations. In fact, 30%–35% of Gen Z young adults reported feeling depressed in 2021–2022.[6] This is also uniquely the generation that has fully been exposed to and has grown up with access to technology, regardless of socioeconomic status. According to the Pew Research Center survey (2022), nearly all Gen Z teens own a smart phone. Unsurprisingly, about half of them (46%) report being online almost constantly. While there are undeniable positives associated with technology for Gen Z, including easy access to information, an overuse of technology, particularly social media, is associated with feelings of isolation. This perpetuates the lack of social skills development, especially in real-life experiences.

Brad Sachs' Non-chronological Model of Launching (2010)

To understand *failure to launch* better, Brad Sachs[7] categorizes young adults who are struggling to achieve independence into five groups: progressing, regrouping, meandering, recovering, and floundering. Each of these categories stands alone and is not necessarily consecutive. Sachs describes a person who is *progressing* as someone who is generally experiencing growth in their pursuit of independence but still needs limited and often temporary parental support to fully meet their responsibilities. For example, a young adult who is pursuing higher education and therefore does not have full-time employment yet and cannot afford all their living expenses without parental support would fall into this category. In the *regrouping* category, young adults have made successive steps/approximations to achieve independence and have demonstrated the ability to lead their own lives but have returned home temporarily to prepare for their next steps of adulthood. These steps may include changing career fields or advancing their current career through further training and living at home to save money while doing so. The *meandering* group is characterized by the young adult making efforts to advance forward in their independence but not quite having a clear direction and, at times, may seem to be regressing back to former stages without much forward momentum. A young adult who holds temporary jobs while in search of the dream job or career would fall under the *meandering* category. The *recovering* category describes young adults who left home and achieved independence for some time but are returning home due to a failed attempt. This could be a young adult who lost their job because of a struggling economy and is unable to find another job to be able to continue to live independently. The *recovering* category is promising, as the young adult can be recognized to have had the minimal skills to try and gain independence for the first try. It is important to identify which category your young adult may fall into, as it can provide a roadmap to identify the skills that are lacking and how to provide the steps to move forward as an independent adult (skills we will discuss in the following chapters).

This book aims to provide a guide toward preventing rather than treating "failure to launch." Therefore, it is important to ask your young adult where they think they are in terms of their preparation and for their caretaker/parent to also assess their stage/progress. Assess yourself or your child as you/they are in the present, not what you/they promise to be in the future.

Family Systems in the United States versus Other Countries and Their Contribution to Multi-generational Family Homes

Due to cultural, economic, and social factors, family systems and the prevalence of multi-generational family homes can vary significantly. The United States is a melting pot of cultures across the world, and it is important to examine when a particular culture may be influencing a young adult's ability to achieve independent success. Cultural attitudes and traditions around family dynamics play a significant role in shaping living arrangements. For example, in some countries, such as many Asian and Middle Eastern cultures, living in multi-generational households is more common and widely accepted. These cultures often place a strong emphasis on certain values such as respect for elders and the responsibility of adult children to take care of their aging parents, whereas independence and self-sufficiency are more emphasized in the United States. Interestingly, cultural trends in the United States (e.g., "helicopter parenting"—parents constantly around—or "tiger parenting"—advocating in place of the child themselves) reinforce parents will continue to take on the role of financial and emotional support well into adulthood (age 30s–70s!!).

Economic conditions can also influence the prevalence of multi-generational family homes. In countries with lower income levels or higher living costs, multi-generational living may be more common as it offers financial benefits, shared expenses, and the pooling of resources. Relatedly, the availability and effectiveness of social safety nets, such as healthcare, retirement benefits, and housing assistance, can impact the need for multi-generational living. In countries with robust social support systems, there might be less pressure for older adults to rely on their adult children for care and financial support. The availability and affordability of housing can also influence living arrangements. In countries with limited affordable housing, multi-generational living might be a practical solution for families to share costs and resources.

From a social psychological perspective, in countries with significant immigration patterns, multi-generational living may be more common as families from different generations, and cultural backgrounds come together for mutual support and preservation of cultural values. Over time, cultural norms and social dynamics can change, leading to shifts in family structures. For example, as more women enter the workforce in some countries, the traditional roles of caregiving and support may evolve, impacting the prevalence of multi-generational homes.

In the United States, multi-generational living has seen a resurgence in recent years, driven by factors such as economic challenges, rising healthcare costs, and changing family dynamics. The Recession of 2008 and the COVID-19 pandemic have also contributed to an increase in multi-generational households, as families sought to navigate economic uncertainties and care for vulnerable family members.[8] These patterns have persisted despite availability of vaccines and lower observed health risks by the Food and Drug Administration. However, despite the growing trend, multi-generational living is still less common in the United States compared to some other countries. Individualism, cultural norms surrounding independence and privacy, and the emphasis on nuclear family units have historically influenced the preference for separate households in the United States.

Overall, the prevalence of multi-generational family homes is shaped by a complex interplay of cultural, economic, and social factors unique to each country and region. As such, it is important to distinguish purposeful multi-generational-living arrangements from gaining successful independence, in that in the latter there is typically a *lack* of contribution to the household whether financially or helping to support family members in other ways (e.g., chores).

Conclusion

Above we have identified several theories, stages of development, and cultural norms/expectations that have contributed to a young adult *not* gaining successful and independent finances, housing, employment, and social goals. We have identified the *problem*. In the marketplace currently, there are a plethora of resources that examine and treat the *problem* of *failure to launch* and how to address it *retroactively* as a parent of a young adult or as the young adult themselves. However, what remains a mystery is how to *prevent failure to launch* in the first place (i.e., how to be *proactive* rather than *reactive*).

New skills acquisition, real-world experience, and applications from a younger age (ages 13–25) are where our book and program differ from the rest. We will explain how we developed our program, which is aimed at increasing a young adult's chances of successful independence in the early and later stages of adulthood through skill acquisition and real-world practice in the younger stages of development (ages 13–25). In other words, engaging with these skills early in life makes a huge impact when it comes time for the actual launching. Learning the skills and following the recommendations in this book will give you or your child a significant, real-world, *advantage* compared to their peers that will help them become a successful and independent young adult.

References

1 Pew Research Center. *Teens, social media and technology 2022*. Washington (DC): Pew Research Center; 2022. Available from: https://www.pewresearch.org/internet/2022/11/

2 Employee Benefit Research Institute (EBRI). *Caregivers and retirement: findings from the 2023 Retirement Confidence Survey (RCS)*. Washington (DC): EBRI; 2023.
3 Dickson JM, Tan V, Huntley CD. Why do we pursue the personal goals we do? The relationships between distinct goal motives and subjective well-being. *J Cross Cult Psychol*. 2025;56(7):797–808.
4 Jacob J, Stanković M, Spuerck I, Shokraneh F. Goal setting with young people for anxiety and depression: what works for whom in therapeutic relationships? A literature review and insight analysis. *BMC Psychol*. 2022;10:171.
5 Arnett J, Fishel E. Getting to 30: a parent's guide to the 20-something years. *J Youth Adolesc*. 2014;43(11):1946–1948.
6 U.S. Census Bureau. *Survey of Income and Program Participation (SIPP), 2022 data release*. Washington (DC): U.S. Census Bureau; 2023.
7 Sachs BE. *Emptying the nest: launching your young adult toward success and self-reliance*. New York (NY): St. Martin's Griffin; 2010.
8 Fry R. *Young adults in the U.S. are much more likely than 50 years ago to be living in a multigenerational household*. Washington (DC): Pew Research Center; 2022 Jul 20.

2 How to Follow the Life-Prep Program

The Basic Psychological Skills Needed to Become a Successful Young Adult

History of Our Program and the Problem We Are Solving

We have spent over 15 years successfully treating young adults who have failed to gain financial, social, housing, and career independence in a clinical, outpatient setting. When a patient first enters treatment, they typically have limited or no motivation, live at home full-time, have no job or job prospects, concurrent mental illness concerns (e.g., anxiety, depression, and executive functioning disorders), and no financial independence. The treatment for those who have not launched successfully not only includes cognitive-behavioral therapy (an evidence-based treatment for anxiety and depression), but several ancillary and equally important executive functioning rehabilitation (e.g., problem-solving and planning skills acquisition), developing realistic goals and expectations, and working with families (i.e., family therapy) to improve treatment follow-through and overall communication.

Years of this work led to innumerable staff discussions examining the variables that not only led our patients to a lack of independence, but more importantly if certain psychological skills had been acquired earlier on in life, they might have lessened these issues if not entirely prevented them! Our program is aimed at preventing the reader from "failing to launch" through a series of psychological skills acquisition and experiential practice over time.

Prevention is the *best* medicine.

An Important Note:

While our program was developed from our work with a clinical population, as a preventative model, it is meant for ALL current and future young adults (ages 13–25), regardless of mental health status.

At What Age Should This Program Be Learned?

We would recommend the program be started anywhere from *13–21 years of age (but can go up to age 30)*. The earlier, the better! The skills you and

DOI: 10.4324/9781003649410-2

your young adult are about to learn in this program not only need to be initially learned/acquired, but they need to be practiced across many years and in a multitude of situations and emotional states. This recommendation is based on over 20 years of clinical experience. It is developmentally appropriate to begin learning and applying these skills as early as the first year of high school. Most young adults do not start seriously considering their future until high school (when the definable goal after high school is either higher education/college, trade school, or employment), but valuable years are then lost to the acquisition and practice of skills that can lead to "launching" successfully. It is important to know how to be able to conduct individual trial-and-error experiments, so the young adult and their support system (i.e., your caregivers/family) know what works in the long-term.

We frequently discuss that this process is *not* about "re-inventing the wheel," but rather learning new skills to fortify your "wheel" so it holds up under many conditions. Think about and discuss the ways your parents/caregivers, siblings/cousins, or friends became successful and independent young adults. Ask them their stories. What mistakes did they make? What successes did they have? The road to independence and success is never straightforward or "one-size-fits all."

Some suggested questions you can ask your support network (e.g., family, friends, teachers, etc.) about their launching experience:

1 Where did you live after college?

   a How did you decide to live in that location? Based on what reasons?
   b How did you pay rent? Did you live on your own or with roommates?
   c How long did it take you to afford rent? How did you save?
   d How did you find a job? Were you happy with your first job?
   e How did you budget yourself?

2 How did you handle your social life after college? What was it like?

   a How did you handle your romantic life and expectations?

3 What did it feel like to have a world of possibilities open to you?
4 How did you narrow down what you wanted as a job or career?
5 How did you manage your relationship with your own parents/caretakers?

   a What was the experience of getting your parents to see you as a young adult?

You may think of even more questions to ask. Remember the more information you have, the better prepared you will be! You can also ask numerous people of different careers and life stages these questions and compare their different launching experiences.

Even if you are 14 years old and these questions may seem years off, it is not about knowing your specific plan and what you are going to do to be independent; it is about acquiring new skills to know how to navigate options once life presents them to you. It may seem as though four years in high school lasts forever, or four years in college is a long time, but it will go by faster than you can believe, and we want you to be prepared.

Overview of Our Life-Prep Program

The following skills were reverse engineered from successfully treating clinical patients who had NOT been able to gain functional independence as a young adult. We found that establishing and practicing these skills as foundational tools in your repertoire will help prepare you in both a specific and applied, more global way, for success. Importantly, the program will prepare you for times when you fail and you will know how to cope successfully with those failures without stalling out or shutting down.

In this chapter, you will be provided with a brief overview of the *Life-Prep program*. You can decide which chapter/skill may be more important for you to start or if you want to begin the program in our recommended order (from Chapters 1–13).

As we have stated above, your life path is not going to be linear (not in a straight line). When we are younger, it seems straightforward. We go to preschool, elementary school, middle school, high school, and then a two- or four-year college or trade school. However, afterwards, it is both exciting and terrifying that there are so many options out there.

Indeed, we frequently hear such statements as (Figure 2.1):

"Which career could I possibly choose?"
"Will I be good at my career?"
"Will I enjoy it?"
"Will it fulfill me in the short and long-term?"
"Will I make enough money to support myself and if I decide to have a family?"

After a two- or four-year college/vocational education, the possibilities are endless, and further decisions can lead to a high level of anxiety and avoidance. The skills we will discuss in our program will help to be able to fortify your defenses. They will help you be able to make these types of decisions and follow through with them in a more thoughtful and meaningful manner (Figure 2.2).

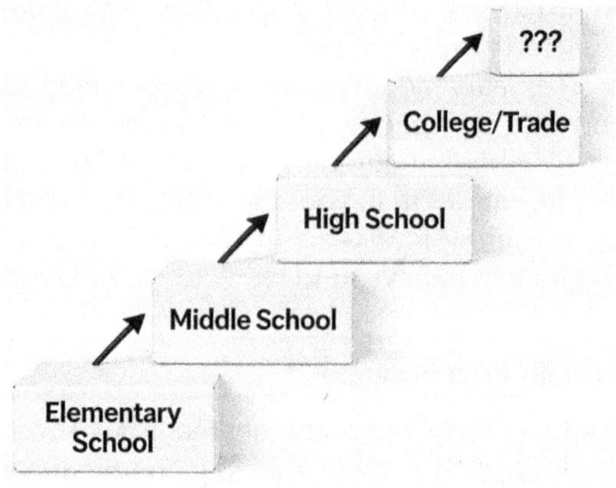

Figure 2.1 A staircase diagram made of labeled blocks shows stages of education progressing upward: Elementary School, Middle School, High School, and College/Trade, ending with a top block labeled with question marks, indicating an uncertain future path.

The Core Components and Brief Review of Our *Life-Prep Program*

Learning Your Strengths, Limitations, and Weaknesses

It is likely that throughout your life you have already been asked to complete the task of examining your strengths, limitations, and weaknesses. However, in Chapter 3, we want you to think of this task very differently. It is not just about what you are good or not good at, it is about deep diving into critical thinking skills and evaluating yourself as an employer or career mentor might do.

We want to encourage you to think "outside the box." What does that mean? Well, as we will discuss in Chapter 3, it means thinking of the items that you *do not* know. Try taking a survey from others about your strengths, limitations, and weaknesses. It is about exploring not only your interests, but how you handle stressors and problems in the long term. For example, let us say "David," a student of engineering, loves numbers and problem-solving, but hates manipulating anything by hand. David wants to be a mechanical engineer, which may require him to be physical with his hands at different points in time (even if not all the time). Should David then reconsider moving to a different major or career? How will his dislike of physically manipulating objects interact with his ability to be a mechanical engineer? We typically do not "deep dive" or "think outside the box" when it comes to our strengths, limitations, and weaknesses, and that is what this program will encourage you to do.

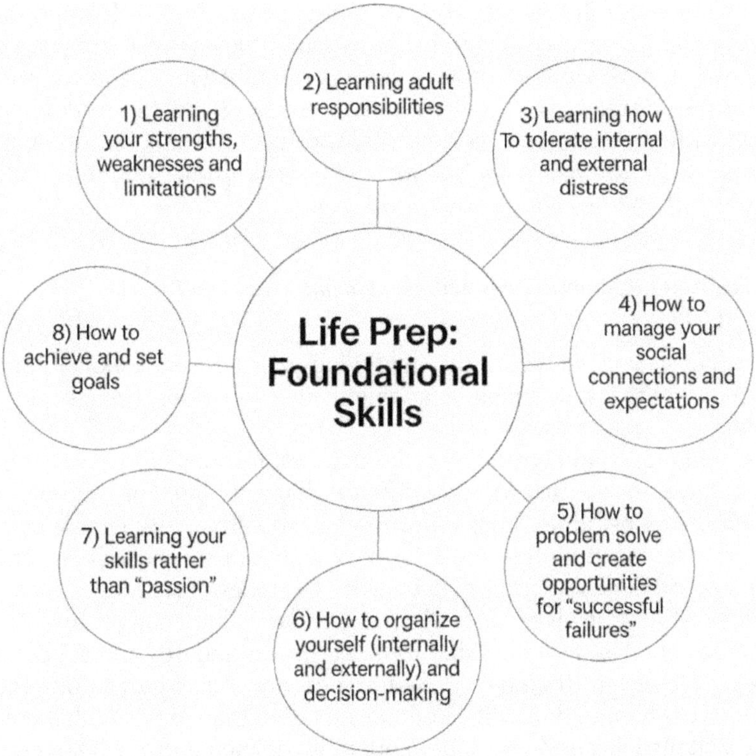

Figure 2.2 A circular diagram titled "Life Prep: Foundational Skills" shows eight connected areas: learning your strengths, weaknesses, and limitations; learning adult responsibilities; learning how to tolerate internal and external distress; managing social connections and expectations; problem solving and creating opportunities from "successful failures"; organizing yourself and making decisions; focusing on skills rather than "passion"; and setting and achieving goals.

We want to challenge how you see yourself in the world. Do you think of yourself as athletic or a good student/intelligent, and how do you measure that? We all have different ways of evaluating ourselves when it comes to our own self-perception. It is important to remember that we may need to re-evaluate our own evaluation system. Many individuals finishing college evaluate themselves by what school they attended or how well they performed in their classes (i.e., Grade Point Average; GPA). However, this system of self-evaluation needs to change once the education process is complete. Imagine how you may feel about yourself once you no longer have grades to gauge your performance? Maybe you will feel free and great, but maybe you will feel lost and without your bearings. It is important to evaluate these systems constantly and whether they are serving you well.

Once you have worked through these current systems of evaluations and then you re-evaluate, you will be able to see how you can re-define your strengths, limitations, and weaknesses. You want to think about what will not only work for you now, but what will work during and after college, and the early part of young adulthood (and further on).

Learning Adult Responsibilities and Recognizing What You Do Not Know in Life

In Chapter 4, you will work on identifying your current responsibilities in the following areas: financial, academic/career/job, household, social, and health.

You will assess and write down the different responsibilities you will expect to have as you pass through different stages of life. For example, how will your responsibilities change from when you are in ninth grade to when you are a senior in high school? Or how will your responsibilities change when you are a freshman in college to a last semester senior?

We can find ourselves falsely believing that as life changes and the expectations change, I will be able to meet those standards and successfully achieve. However, there are no guarantees, and it is better to understand the types of changes that will be occurring rather than to "go with the flow."

We will also discuss what independent living means and what it consists of (e.g., costs of living, geographical locations, social responsibilities, living alone vs. with someone else, taxes, retirement, etc.). The purpose of Chapter 4 is to bring these components into the forefront of your awareness so you can work on how, when, and where you want to start approaching them.

It is equally important to know what you *do NOT* know as well. We address questions that encourage you to think in ways that you have not done previously. We will have you work on identifying skills (e.g., resources for information, social discussions with those who have gained functional independence prior to you, etc.) to help you discover the questions you did not know you needed to ask.

Learning How to Tolerate Internal and External Distress

In Chapter 5, you will learn how to tolerate both internal and external distress. When we are growing up, it is very common for our caretakers to assume responsibility for our distress. For example, if you are a small toddler and you fall and cut your knee, your caretaker may hug you, give you positive words of comfort, and then bandage you up. Hugging and the verbal words of comfort are meant to reduce your internal distress, and the bandage is meant to reduce any pain or external distress you have experienced. Though this is expected as a young child, it is actually more common than not for caretakers to assume these responsibilities and send a young adult off in life without them developing these skills independently.

In this program, you will learn to identify internal distress (i.e., the emotions you experience that are difficult to cope with internally such as surprise, nervousness, anger, anxiety, sadness, etc.) as well as the external situations you find difficult to manage on your own (e.g., making an appointment at a doctor's office or speaking with a teacher about your grade, buying a house, etc.). In this regard, we are going to teach you and review several skills to accomplish these tasks independently: acceptance, problem-solving, and grounding skills to reduce high levels of different emotions (e.g., anger, anxiety). We will discuss the following in order to cope with uncomfortable levels of emotion: emotional thermometer assessment (mindfulness and awareness training), progressive muscle relaxation, self-soothing/emotional grounding techniques, engaging in a physically competing activity to disengage and not avoid the emotion, moving physically away from the source of stress, and challenging how you are thinking about the stressor (whether internal or external).

Learning How to Manage Your Social Connections and Expectations

In Chapter 6, you will learn how to manage your social relationships and expectations related to those relationships (e.g., how many friends will you have and what your frequency of contact will be as you get older and life-circumstances change). You will break down your network of friends, family, teachers/bosses/supervisors, romantic partners into even more distinct categories. As we get older, our relationships naturally change. When we are younger, they can form by being near someone else (i.e., physical proximity), but as we get older, we add several variables that determine whether we develop a social connection with someone else (e.g., common interests). It is important to think about whether you expect all your relationships to be close or how you want to balance working relationships, close relationships, intimate relationships, and acquaintances.

We will also explore what your priorities are for your relationships at different stages of your life (e.g., middle school, high school, college, post-college/job experience, and adulthood). At different stages of our lives, we have more or less time for others and ourselves. We can have different priorities. There is no *one* way to do it *right,* however, there are ways that will be wrong for *you*. Interactions or lack of interactions you have can lead you to have helpful or unhelpful thoughts or positive or negative feelings. We will explore what a path for you can look like.

Using Your Executive Functioning Skills Effectively and Opportunities for Successful Failures

In Chapter 7, you will learn how to use executive functioning skills (e.g., problem-solving) as well as giving yourself opportunities for "successful failures." We will examine how to identify a "problem," and when you can let it be naturally solved on its own or whether it needs a proactive plan. We address breaking down larger problems into smaller, subsets of problems to be solved over a designated period of time that can be approached with more confidence and less intimidation.

When we feel overwhelmed by the immensity of a problem, it can cause us to freeze or we avoid it entirely. If we do not know how to break it down into manageable pieces, giving us forward momentum, we can find it very difficult to make progress toward achieving the larger, overall goal. We can also think of a helpful and realistic timetable to follow. Developing a realistic timetable is something that is difficult to do, as most of us will think we can do MORE than we can, and if we are unable to meet that goal, we may feel poorly about ourselves. Sometimes, what gets in our way is how the problem makes us *feel*. In this chapter, we will explore several techniques used to reduce our overall stress and increase our focus and ability to engage with the problem at hand. These include deep breathing techniques, progressive muscle relaxation, acceptance and mindfulness strategies, and challenging our unhelpful thinking.

In our program, our skills are heavily focused on encouraging you to use them independently before reaching out to anyone else for assistance. While we do encourage getting assistance from others as a *last resort*, we want your first, second, third, and fourth attempts at solving a problem to rely on your *own* skills and thought processes. This is encouraging a concept in psychology known as self-efficacy (our ability to know that we, ourselves, have the internal and external skills to successfully cope).

We will also explore opportunities for "successful failures." First, we define what a "successful failure" is and why it is important. Successful failures are opportunities we know we will likely fail at completing. Why are these so important? Well, because life hands them to us regardless of whether we want them or not and we need to know how to cope.

You may have heard the terms "helicopter parenting" or "snowplow parenting." "Helicopter parenting" is when parents hover over their children to direct them to statistically make the best decision, reducing their opportunities to fail. "Snowplow parenting" is when a parent will plow all the snow (i.e., all adversities in life) for the child/young adult, therefore not allowing them the opportunities to problem-solve themselves. Our program will help you approach situations you will likely fail at and to practice using your *own* coping strategies.

Decision-Making and Organizational Skills

In Chapter 8, we address how to make effective and easily implemented decisions and systems by which you currently organize yourself. Decision-making skills rely heavily on us not avoiding the problem at hand. Underneath the umbrella of problem-solving lies decision-making and organizational skills.

We cover the ways to categorize a decision to be made (e.g., financial, educational, location, etc.), and what benefits or consequences this has for you within a particular timeframe (e.g., immediately vs. six-months vs. two years from now). We review the pros and cons of deciding while also tolerating the uncertainty of not knowing if it is the "perfect" decision to make. We also address how to find the motivation to follow through on a decision.

In addition, we examine the organizational system you already have and ones that you may want to adapt over time. How we organize our mind and our external world (e.g., our bedroom, work calendar, icons on your phone, etc.) is not a one-size-fits-all approach. We take a deep dive into different types of organizational systems to assess the effectiveness of your current system and how changes to that system may help your decision-making and problem-solving skills. The more effective these skills are, the more likely you are to succeed as a young adult who can adapt their systems, rather than giving up altogether.

Using Your Skills Rather than Passion to Determine Life Satisfaction

In Chapter 9, we focus on using your *skills* rather than *passion* to determine your life satisfaction. As clinicians, something we hear all too often is "I am so passionate about [this] or [that]." However, we discuss the limitations of how *passion* can only get you so far, in that it waxes and wanes over time and can be very inconsistent. A more consistent way to determine your life satisfaction (i.e., achieving a level of satisfaction approximately averaging 60% of the time), is through the betterment and use of your current skills and planning toward *mastery* over future skills.

We encourage you to value your current repertoire of skills, how to gain mastery over them, and how to learn what new skills you want in the future. We will examine how your skills will translate on a realistic level (e.g., how your skills can lead into a job or a career). Rather than your passion, it is your <u>skills</u> that more consistently determine your life satisfaction and success as a young adult and the years following.

How to Set and Achieve Your Goals

In Chapter 10, our aim is to be able to have you design "life goals" in a realistic and achievable way. We will help you define what a *dream* versus a *goal* is. We will work on how to structure your time and effort to achieve your goal. Goals can be in many different areas of life. For example, what are your educational goals? Financial goals? Housing goals? We also want your goals to be realistic and for you to set your pacing in a realistic way toward those goals.

In this chapter, we help you devise a plan to help achieve your goal/s and ways to break your overall goal/s into subsets of goals. Goals are frequently not reached because when our first attempt goes wrong, we tend to give that goal up. We will discuss tolerating uncertainty, making the potential wrong decision, and how to stick with your goals despite not reaching the smaller goals or making wrong decisions.

Overall, some would refer to the ability to stick with your goals despite experiencing something unpleasant (e.g., not achieving a smaller goal on the path to the larger goal) as "stick-to-it-iveness." This chapter devotes time on how you can learn to regroup (i.e., forming new goals, a new timeline, challenging your thoughts and feelings about re-grouping, and developing a larger, new plan toward the initial goal). These skills help to build what is called "resilience." Resilience can be defined as the ability to recover and regroup after facing a difficult situation or experience. Building an adequate level of resiliency is optimal in young adulthood as you will face many obstacles that can feel discouraging and overwhelming at times.

How to Use This Program

It is recommended that you follow the skills in sequential order of each chapter as listed. Each skills-based chapter builds upon the previous one. However, we also recognize that time and relevance are always a consideration, so it is possible (though not the recommended first option), to start at a chapter (or skill) that is most important or pressing to you.

Due to some of the concepts being more sophisticated, we make the following age-based recommendations for the consumption of this program:

Ages 13–15

Read/practice this program as a young adult *in combination with* a parent/caregiver

Ages 16–30

Program can be consumed *alone* or in *combination with* a parent/caregiver

All parents/caregivers can consume the program and work on it with their young adult (13–31).

If you want Dr. Johanna Kaplan herself lead you through these skills, feel free to participate in the online Life-Prep Program, complete with homework and demonstration videos (https://www.lifeprep.studio)

3 Defining Strengths, Weaknesses, and Limitations

We want you to assess what you currently consider your strengths, weaknesses, and limitations. Think of how you, and only you, define these terms. According to your own definitions, fill out the paragraphs below. As you start to read the remainder of the chapter, you will be asked to fill this out again and make comparisons.

Write down a five-sentence paragraph about your strengths, weaknesses, and limitations

____
____
____
____
____
____
____
____
____

Generally, strengths are thought of as activities or skills in which a person excels, while weaknesses, however, are the opposite. Weaknesses are viewed through a negative lens, in that, skills (or lack thereof) in which a person does not excel are not viewed positively. We seek to change and, most importantly, challenge these definitions going forward in your life. Why do strengths have to be viewed positively and weaknesses negatively? Skills we have obtained and are by definition, "good at" need to be maintained with a humble approach; otherwise, we risk losing those skills. Anyone can become "too big for their own boots," as the saying goes. Is it possible for us to view weaknesses more similarly to strengths? As in, can we see them both as continuous goals throughout our life?

When initially thinking of strengths and weaknesses, it can be very polarizing. Let's use "Jose" as a case example. Jose grew up in southern Texas,

DOI: 10.4324/9781003649410-3

on the Mexican border. His parents immigrated to the United States in the 1980s from Ecuador. Jose was consistently reinforced that the language he spoke with his family, Spanish, was well learned. However, when Jose began taking Spanish classes in school, he learned that while he knew he could speak well, he did not know how to properly write Spanish. He learned that he still needed to improve an area he had previously thought to be a strength. Just like Jose, we can become accustomed to being comfortable in a skill we think we have mastered but can become quickly humbled by needing to maintain or strengthen the already "strong" skill.

The same could also be said for a weakness. Let's learn from "Charlotte." Charlotte believes that she is "horrible" at playing tennis but surprised herself in a match against a higher-level player. The other player was ranked higher and therefore, defined by the league as a better player. However, Charlotte played consistently, and all her balls went in while the other player was getting frustrated and hitting the ball out/losing points. She was surprised to win the match, having perceived herself as the weaker player. She learned she was able to play with a skill she placed in the "weakness" category and win the match.

The lesson here is sometimes what is perceived as a weakness can be a strength and what is a strength can also sometimes be a weakness. Try and apply this principle for yourself today. Ask your friends and family during a meal what strength is a weakness and what weakness can be a strength.

Another variable that needs to be considered is limitations. We are not all equal. We all have advantages and disadvantages that are beyond our control or reach, at times. This could be financial background or available resources, support system access, access to a quality education, and any variables out of a person's control. None of us are immune from limitations, whether it is socioeconomic, income, race-based, gender-based, etc. Again, none of these in and of themselves are limitations, but when we look at society, we are nowhere close to equality. We absolutely need to include these factors into the equation.

When working with a population that is in their early 20s, our clinical observations have been that they are overly optimistic and need more realism. For example, when discussing with a high school auditorium of freshman-seniors and asking them the percentage of taxes taken out of a paycheck, the collective answers ranged from 3% to 6%. Just so you know, taxes (state and federal combined) can range from anywhere (from 15% to 55%). Generally, high schools and colleges do not talk about state and federal tax rates when it comes to choosing a school or a career. That can be due to several factors, including socioeconomic or financial status. Of note, we recently were informed of a medical physician who chose employment in a lower-taxed state although they were offered more money in a higher-taxed state. Once they realized their net income would be higher due to the lower tax rates, despite making less money, it influenced their decision. This is the type of thinking we are encouraging when discussing "limitations." We want to encourage more "outside the box" thinking.

What does "outside the box" thinking mean? It means looking at our definitions and challenging them, as we did above. It also means examining how these definitions might change over time. We want to encourage everyone to think: while these are my strengths, weaknesses, and limitations now in my life, what will they be five or ten years in the future? Most of you reading this will be a few years from graduating high school or college (or any post-high school training). What do you think about your future and how to plan? How do you self-evaluate? How much will life change in two, five, or ten years?

Academic/Employment Concerns (Ages 22–24)

We want to start this section with an example to help demonstrate the experiences you could have in your early 20s in the academic/employment realm. For example, you find that after self-evaluating your strengths, weaknesses, and limitations (in general), you determine you are very proficient in social skills. Making new friends or introducing yourself to teachers or your peers has always been a rather easy task. However, as written above, we want to be able to always question our own strengths. Maybe you have been able to make friends easily because you have been in environments (e.g., school) where you are around people of similar age and interests. When you graduate college, your co-workers will likely range from peers your age to up to 55 years older than you. You may find yourself not able to relate to them on typical interests of those in your generation. Think of all the social media posts on the differences between Generation Z vs. Millennials. These generational gaps make it harder to socially relate to someone in a different generation. It is not impossible, but it is more difficult. When you are 22–24 years of age and starting your career, whether it be in a job or more schooling, you will need to interact with people of different generations. It is a safe bet to assume that what you learned from your peers is not going to apply to everyone around you. What may have been an area of strength for you, you will now need to amend and work on to adapt to a different set of peers.

We want you to think of your caretakers (whether a parent, friend, grandparent). What generation they are in now and how they might handle a friendly interaction or a conflict? Typically, most supervisors tend to be a generation prior to the current one. How might it help you to know how to interact in a professional way with someone in that generation? For example, if you started off a sentence with "Bruh…" how might that be received? Or how would it be perceived if you ask your supervisor why you did not get ALL positive remarks on your yearly review? Remember, different generations do not give positive feedback like others do, and this is just one variable of which to be aware.

Sometimes what is needed is an understanding of another person, their perspective, and how to optimize your communication with them. Ask others around you (especially those of different genders, sexes, cultural backgrounds, religious beliefs, and ages) how they would like to be addressed. Is there a better approach or better phrasing to use? There is no need to reinvent the wheel every time. Asking others about their approach to what works vs. what does not, especially for them, is a great place to start.

It is also important to recognize that while you may have a bachelor's or medical degree, it does not mean you get the "top of the pyramid" job to start. Across all professions, you will deal with adversity. Even being the "boss" or a supervisor does not equate to power or an easy life. Understanding this process is not straightforward, and understanding that it can be a difficult journey, sometimes harder and sometimes easier, is par for the course.

Social Concerns (Ages 22–24)

When you are 22/23 years of age, post-college, what will life be like and how do your strengths, weaknesses, and limitations affect your life? It is important to recognize that up until this point, you have been physically surrounded by most of your friends much of the day, for most days of the week. This is because you completed activities or events with them (e.g., school, sport, club). When you enter the "real world," you will not be surrounded by friends all the time. This can make you feel isolated and alone. Considering strengths and weaknesses here, how well do you handle being alone? Can you go out to a restaurant and eat alone? Can you be satisfied without being social with friends over a weekend? You want to work on being comfortable with yourself and in your own company first and foremost. It can be difficult listening to your own thoughts and not being distracted by others around you, but it is also a great opportunity to continue to get to know yourself.

Physical Concerns (Ages 22–24)

What our physical body is capable of changes at different ages. It is not necessarily good or bad to have a body that changes over time. A lot of our capabilities and our health depend on environmental factors, like the decisions we make and how we treat our body. Do you use illegal drugs or overuse alcohol? When you are younger, the effects are not as apparent, but when you get older, the use you had when you were younger finally takes a toll. Look at rock stars in their 70s compared to when they were in their 20s, and if they were open about using substances, you can visually see the effects. Make sure you take good care of your body; it is the only one you will have going into the future. When we are younger, it is very hard to imagine ourselves 20 years down the road, but if you take care of your body now, in 20 years you will be happy you did.

We are also not guaranteed a pristine body to start. Many of us have physical disabilities or limitations that impact our decision-making in the present and future. For example, if you are born with a genetic disorder that limits your muscle mass, you may not be the best fit for becoming a firefighter. However, that does not mean you cannot become a volunteer or administrator in the firefighter department. Thinking creatively is the key to achieving your goals in a realistic way (will be discussed in Chapter 10).

Religiosity/Belief System (Ages 22–24)

Psychologists, psychiatrists, and mental health practitioners have long observed and recorded religious and spiritual beliefs provide excellent coping mechanisms when a person is dealing with a myriad of mental health concerns, such as depression or anxiety.1 What we have not focused on, though, is that these beliefs rapidly alter throughout our childhood and young adulthood. It is not our place to recommend or choose a faith or belief system for you, but it is our place to demonstrate that those who do have strong religious beliefs or a faith system do purport to feel supported during perilous times in their life (e.g., feeling anxious or depressed). We encourage you to explore different belief systems or even to broaden your current one. Focus on how you can utilize your system, while being held accountable to yourself and others to have compassion and to love yourself. It sounds difficult, but these "protective" factors can truly help, especially when life is hard and you are on your own without an immediately available support system. We want to encourage you to ponder how your beliefs/non-beliefs play into your assessment of your strengths, weaknesses, and limitations.

Are You Thinking More Holistically?

Now that we have gotten you to think of yourself in a more holistic manner, can you now re-assess your strengths, weaknesses, and limitations in the social, academic/job, physical, and religion/belief domains? Use all the various points that we discussed above to complete this task.

See below for the charts. Make sure to take your time filling them out. You can fill them out with your support system or by yourself.

What are your *strengths* in each domain:

Social:

Academic:

Physical:

Religion/Belief System:

Random Interests:

What are your *weaknesses* in each domain:

Social:

Academic:

Physical:

Religion/Belief System:

Random Interests:

What are your *limitations* in each domain:

Social:

Academic:

Physical:

Religion/Belief System:

Random Interests:

____
____
____
____

Now that you have completed the worksheets above, fill in the following statement again. Afterward, go back to the original statement you wrote at the beginning of the chapter and compare the two responses.

Take the time to re-write your new statement and compare it to the first one you wrote:

Write down a *new* five-sentence paragraph about your *strengths, weaknesses, and limitations*:

____
____
____
____
____
____
____
____

How are these two five-sentence paragraphs similar or different? Have you seen growth? We hope so, but if the answer is "no," we encourage you to go back and fill in each worksheet again. Really challenge your baseline definitions of your strengths, weaknesses, and limitations according to the expanded definitions above.

Evidence-Based Support of Self-evaluation

When we self-examine, we tend to be either too permissive (relaxed) or too critical of ourselves. It is important to be objective in our subjective assessment of ourselves. What that means is considering several influential variables, such as grit, accountability, and perseverance. We will get into the latter two variables when we discuss goal setting and goal keeping/follow-through. However, we wanted to take the self-evaluation angle as an opportunity to let you evaluate your own level of "grit" and insight.

What is *grit*? Is the grit between your teeth after a meal? Well, in a sense, maybe? Think of that leftover food that gets stuck in your teeth, maybe a popcorn kernel? It's stubborn, refuses to come out, and really wedges itself in there nice and tight. Our own grit helps us to combine our own interests (some term this "passion" but as we will discuss later why we are not fans of the word "passion") and perseverance (a term of which we are huge fans).

Grit is not just your interests, your wishes or hopes, but also your perseverance, and concrete skills like accountability, follow-through, and setting up realistic short- and long-term goals. These are all areas our book will address. If you can achieve a substantial level of grit (you will know what yours is when you achieve a hard-earned, long-term goal), then you will have a generally high rate of success in the goals you set for yourself.[1–4] Many different fields have applied this theory. For example, in weight management a person must develop short- and long-term goals that are realistic. However, and more importantly, there will absolutely be times (short or extended) when you will falter on these goals. You will have bad days. So, having grit means accepting that and then developing a plan to which you can push through to motivate yourself and get back on track and keep with the plan.

We want you to have a realistic insight into your own strengths, weaknesses, and limitations so you will have the ability to follow through in the long-term and succeed upon entering young adulthood. At the same time, we want you to be thinking outside the box and to be flexible in what it means to be "successful." The opportunities are limitless!

References

1 Aggarwal S, Wright J, Morgan A, et al. Religiosity and spirituality in the prevention and management of depression and anxiety in young people: a systematic review and meta-analysis. *BMC Psychiatry*. 2023;23:729.
2 Cormier DL, Dunn JG, Dunn JC. Examining the domain specificity of grit. *Pers Individ Dif.* 2019;139:349–354.
3 Crede M, Tynan M, Harms P. Much ado about grit: a meta-analytic synthesis of the grit literature. *J Pers Soc Psychol.* 2017;113(3):492–511.
4 Vinothkumar M, Prasad N. Moderating role of resilience in the relationship between grit and psychological well-being. *Int J Psychol Psychiatry.* 2016;4(2):10.

4 Learning Adult Responsibilities

Just as you learned how to reconceptualize (or think of in a different way) your strengths, weaknesses, and limitations, we will also guide you through taking the next steps to learning adult responsibilities. As our chapters progress, you will start to see some overlap in skills and recommendations for implementation. We are doing this on purpose. We want you to implement these skills *consistently* in your daily life.

As a child, your caregivers may have had you engage in tasks or chores to help you begin to learn adult responsibilities. Below is a chart that we have recommended to our patients depending on their age. The purpose of engaging in these activities (whether a reward was received) is to build distress tolerance, progressive more advancing independent-living skill sets, and to work toward mastery over "adult-like" responsibilities. Glance over the chart below and depending on your age, assess whether you have already mastered (consistently completed many times over at least a six-month period) these responsibilities. We have included chores/responsibilities that were to be completed at a younger age to also give you a sense of how you have progressed over time. We have seen that the best predictor of future behavior is past behavior. Thus, if you have moved rather slowly through acquisition of these skills over time, chances are the same pace will continue without the type of interventions recommended in this book.

Chore/Responsibility Acquisition at Different Ages

- **2–4-year-olds**
  - Help dust
  - Put napkins on table
  - Help put away toys
  - Put laundry in hamper
  - Help feed pets

DOI: 10.4324/9781003649410-4

- **4–7-year-olds**
  - Set the table or help set the table
  - Put away toys/things
  - Help feed pets
  - Water plants
  - Put laundry in the hamper
  - Dishes in the dishwasher
  - Help garden
  - Help put away groceries
- **8–10-year-olds**
  - Make your own bed every day
  - Water plants
  - Clean room with direction
  - Set the table
  - Clear the table
  - Dust or vacuum
  - Feed pets
  - Help make dinner
  - Put laundry in hamper
  - Help wash the car
  - Help wash dishes
  - Help load/empty dishwasher
  - Rake leaves
  - Take out the trash
- **11–13-year-olds**
  - Take garbage outside
  - Set the table
  - Clear the table
  - Clean room with direction
  - Put away groceries
  - Clean the bathroom with direction
  - Clean the kitchen
  - Dust, vacuum, mow lawn, feed pets, water plants, put laundry in hamper, help with laundry, and eventually start doing own laundry
  - Help make dinner/make small meals on own, help wash the car/wash car, make bed, help with yard work, shovel snow, wash dishes/load or empty dishwasher

- **14—18-year-olds**
  - All the above, AND
  - Make arrangements to and from school (whether with parent or not)
  - Complete homework independently
  - Speak and advocate to teachers on your own
  - Make your own lunch, take showers, clean the room, and be able to effectively clean the house with the correct cleaners (e.g., wood cleaner for the wood, floor cleaner and mop for the floor, etc.)
  - Learn how their car works (roughly and how to change a flat tire)
  - Know the process of addressing a physical or household emergency
  - Caring for a pet completely on your own
  - Buying groceries
  - How to do laundry independently
  - How to make doctor's appointments for themselves and keep track of their own schedule

- **18—22-year-olds**
  - All the above, AND
  - Design and make your own schedule, whether for work or college
  - Have a part, full, or internship work placement where your supervisor is not a family member
  - Advocate for yourself first in all situations (roommate, professor, and supervisor at work). Do not involve your support system unless it emergently requires it.
  - Do all laundry, clean, schedule yourself to arrive on time to appointments.

The above are *some of the types* of chores (not completely inclusive) that should be completed and mastered at the different ages and stages of development. However, they differ significantly from the responsibilities that you will need to acquire at the ages of 22/23. We will work together below to see how they break down into the following categories: financial, academic/career/job, household, social, and health.

Financial Responsibilities

Around this age (22–23/24), you are either graduating college/university, or you are moving from trade profession training into a more independent career role. Either path leads to the same place, which is substantially more financial responsibility. Some caregivers will help with the initial costs of becoming an adult, but most do not. First, you should have an honest and respectful discussion with your caregivers, engaging them on if they would be willing to help you financially. However, recognize it is not their responsibility to help you financially at this stage of your life. You now need to be responsible for taking care of several financial commitments: taxes, rent, mortgage, healthcare costs, and costs of daily living (e.g., groceries, travel to and from work, car maintenance, and extraneous purchases such as clothing, social activities, and vacations). Most 22–24-year-olds we have worked with significantly underestimate the costs of what it will take to maintain an independent financial lifestyle.

As of the year 2026, rent in a metropolitan area (we will use New York City, NYC, in this case), with a roommate is $3,500 per person, per month (rent total for two people is around $7,000–7,500). This would be a "middle of the road" estimate (not too high, not too low). A lower estimate for living outside Manhattan in Brooklyn or the Williamsburg area, would be approximately $2,400–3,000 per person; living in an expensive area of NYC (e.g., midtown) would range from $5,000–7,000 per month (per person, not in total). Depending on how many rooms or how many people you have living with you, the cost can increase or decrease. Further, you cannot just put down the first month's rent. You need an application, which will consist of proof of your employment status, what you make on a yearly and monthly basis, and one month's rent as a downpayment/deposit. Your first payment is double your monthly rent.

The cost of housing (whether owning or renting) is expected to be approximately 30%–35% of your income. So, in the example above, rent for the entire year would be $42,000 + $3,500 for the deposit (if the monthly rent is $3,500). If rent is at least 30% of your income, and if you want to live in Manhattan (NYC), you need to make at least $151,666 as your yearly salary. As a reality check, that is a large sum to earn directly from undergraduate school or early on in your career. After graduation, the average 22/23-year-old makes around $68,000 their first year. This level is higher for majors in engineering/sciences ($85k), but less for humanities majors ($45–55k).[1]

Now, it gets even more complicated. Remember that the $151,666 a year is not yours in full. You also need to account for taxes (both state and federal) and to pay someone to do your taxes, if you are not knowledgeable. Paying someone to do your taxes can be anywhere from $200 to $2,000 for individual returns. If we are to use New York as an example, first you need to know if you are filing individually or as a family. We will assume that for most of you, an individual filing will be appropriate at this stage of life but do keep in mind this can change when you are legally married and when you have dependents (e.g., children). Second, and likely most important, is understanding how much money will be taken out of your baseline salary for taxes. Let us assume you are working for someone else, and you would file a "W–2" (a legal form/designation indicating your employer pays a portion of your taxes). You will still have federal and state taxes to pay on top of your employer's coverage. A rough estimate is calculated by your tax status (e.g., W–2), your salary level (high salary, higher tax rate), and what state you are living in (certain states have higher income taxes than others and some have none). Using the example above, your federal tax would be approximately 20% and your state is 6%. So, in total, your salary now dips from $151,666 to $112,233. Taxes can change each year based on what your deductions are, what laws have been passed in the federal and state-wide government, salary increases/decreases, your tax status (e.g., filing jointly) and if you move states. Yes, it is a lot to manage, and this is why a lot of people employ actual accountants to file their taxes.

Keeping with the example above, you now have $112,233 with which to pay the remainder of your expenses (including rent). We calculated the average expenses per month in Manhattan among the following:

1 Two-bedroom (shared with another roommate) apartment rent—$3,792.00 (includes deposit spread across 12 months)
2 Utilities (A/C, heat, electricity, water, internet, cable, trash, laundry)—total is $360–400 (split between roommate is $130–200)
3 Groceries/food/dining out—$400–700 per month on groceries; $200–600 per month for going out to a mid-level restaurant 2–4x a month
4 Clothing-$100–400 per month (on average, every month you won't necessarily spend, but holiday months you may spend more)
5 Recreation (movies, gym memberships, outings with friends)—$200–600 per month

Calculating the above expenses on a conservative end (spending the lowest amount) is $4,822 per month and $6,292 on the highest. After accounting for these total expenditures, your actual take-home would be the following: $112,233 (after taxes)-expenditures (above) = $36,729 (remainder if spent moderate-high) $54,369 (remainder if you had low spending). How surprised are you by this? Now, we do have to factor in that Manhattan/NYC is one of the most expensive cities in the world, but not the most (e.g., Paris, London, Los Angeles, San Francisco, and even parts of Chicago are more expensive).

Another large consideration that was not factored into the above equations is saving for your retirement and health care costs. We did not include these in the above because a lot of employers will help to cover these costs for you. However, if they do not, it is important for you to factor these into your budget. Between saving for retirement and healthcare costs every month, the range could be from $600 to $2,500 per month. Investing in your health (as now required by U.S. law, every citizen must have health insurance, or you pay a large fine) and your future is a smart and necessary decision. Your retirement investment can seem so far off in the distance, and while the amount accumulates over time, you will find time passing by much quicker than it did in your schooling days. You do not want to wait to invest in yourself when the time has already passed, and retirement is no longer a realistic option. This effect is called the Proportional Theory of Time proposed by Paul Janet in the late 19th century. According to this theory, because so many milestones (e.g., getting driver's license, graduating) happen before 22/23 years of age, we tend to create stronger memories, and time will feel as though it is moving slower.[2] Also, 10/20 years of your life is still half your life, as opposed to when you are 80 and 40 years is half your life. We want to caution here that time can have a "runaway" effect.[3] Before you know it, you will be 45, and what will you have done to invest in your future?

There are many ways to invest in your future, but we recommend speaking to a financial planner. The human resource manager at your employer should be able to walk you through investments in their company such as 401ks. However, if they are not knowledgeable ask friends or family for a trusted resource for you to speak with about starting your investments. Starting this process when you are 22/23 gives you more time and flexibility and your future self will be thanking you.

Academic/Career/Job Responsibilities

Twenty years ago, first or second year college students, or 18-year-olds moving on to a trade profession, had a few years to "figure it out." The purpose behind general education requirements and not going to a "tech" school or tech college meant that a person had one to two years to figure out what they wanted to major in and what they wanted their future career to be. However, with the fast pace of the world and the introduction of social media and artificial intelligence, by the time we turn 20 most of us are already either barely on track toward those goals or behind. Therefore, we recommend starting as early as possible. Instead of spending your time JUST taking classes your first two years after high school (college or trade school), use this time as an opportunity to apply for internships for on-the-job experience, develop relationships with professors, and engage proactively with as many areas and professions you are interested in (e.g., clubs, organizations). The purpose is to narrow your focus down as soon as possible.

The quicker you narrow your focus, the faster you can engage in internships and get possible job offers after graduation. Many patients we work with wait to apply for their first job after graduation, but by that time they are competing with peers who have interned there for years and have already developed a good reputation. In the end, who would you hire? The person who had demonstrated effort and had developed relationships with your staff and learned all about the job already or someone brand new? The brand-new person would have to be extraordinary to exclude someone in-house for employment. This happens at both lower and higher levels of employment. For example, when companies recruit for CEO's, they are legally required to publicly advertise, however, choosing someone in-house is a preferential trend.

Additionally, it is very important to remember that while your interests, or your "passion" (to be discussed in Chapter 9) may lead you to a certain career, you also want to be sure that the career or job you chose is in line with either the lifestyle you are accustomed to, a lifestyle you aspire to, or one in which you are truly comfortable having as a minimum. For example, you may have come from an upper-middle-class household and live in a nice suburban area. You truly desire to become an actor at local theater. Your caregiver has told you they emotionally support you, but regardless of your choices of career, at the end of college/age 22, they will no longer financially support you. Therefore, you now need to make some difficult decisions. Where will you live? Can you live at home? Will it be free or require rent? Can you afford to live with a roommate? In what area? Will your job pay enough to live? Do you need a second job to make ends meet? If you are making $48,000 (without taxes being taken out yet), what can you afford? The reality is that your lifestyle will be significantly impacted by your salary.

As you can see above, these are not easy responsibilities. These are truly "grown-up" responsibilities. Now, you must be responsible for yourself. No one is expected to come in and save you. Even if they offer or can, there is so much value to achieving your own true independence.

Household Responsibilities

Beyond the utilities and the rent, managing an apartment, a condo, townhouse, house, farm, etc., requires a great deal of responsibility and hard work. Let us speak to renting an apartment first. Some apartments have a landlord/s that manages care of the apartment, and whether this is the case is important to establish at the outset of the lease. Not all landlords cover expenses and not all of them are responsive to issues that develop. Maintenance of a property, even one that is rented, is expected of the renter. These responsibilities can include mowing the lawn, unclogging the drains of hair, cleaning the stove, placing a mousetrap if needed, and many more. These are some of the activities you would not think you might be responsible for as a renter, but you absolutely will be. Again, discuss with your landlord what they will help with and what they will also financially cover; it is usually only the bigger items (e.g., washer/dryer is broken).

As a homeowner, your responsibility amplifies. Around 45%–50% of millennials continue to rent and the other half own. While many Gen Z'ers aspire to own homes, only 25% currently do.[4] Many young adults are starting to weigh the pros and cons in ownership and whether the work is truly a time and financial investment for them personally.4 As opposed to car vehicles, homes tend to appreciate over time (get more valuable), so owning allows you to invest in yourself as opposed to renting, which is investing in someone else's financial future. However, you must put in the work and responsibility of home ownership, which at times can be frustrating, stressful, time-consuming, but also extremely rewarding. We bring up these pros and cons because you need to truly think through them. Did you know that when you get a house inspected, surprises will still await you in home ownership? Homes are like our human bodies; they are flawed. Take your time and think through this process. Several people utilize home ownership as their future retirement investment. They plan to pay off the mortgage and sell the house at a profit. This can be a very smart idea, depending on the profitability of that specific market.

Social Responsibilities

As we mentioned earlier in the book, after we are finished with formal schooling (assuming here you do not pursue continued, advanced degrees), making friends can become more difficult. When peers of your similar age and similar interests are not consistently within your physical proximity, it makes it more difficult to make new friends. You need to be more proactive. Even if you have a roommate or two, make sure to join clubs (e.g., sporting clubs that are university-based exist in major metropolitan cities) to expand your social network.

It will also now be your responsibility to develop new social connections and networks with people of different stages of life compared to you. You can work with anyone ranging from a young parent or older former retiree and your way of relating to people of a different age, culture, gender, or sexual preference/identity, career stage/level, etc. may be something you need time to get educated in and feel comfortable. Take the time to learn. Be patient with yourself and respectful to others. This is your new responsibility. Be open to learning and listening to others' knowledge and experience. You can learn a lot by truly listening.

Another important social responsibility is to learn to be comfortable alone. At this stage in your life, you have either been around your family, classmates, siblings, or friends most of the time, and you have had less experience being truly alone. Going forward as an adult, you will have more time alone. To not become socially isolated (and depressed or anxious), try and allow yourself time and repetitive experiences to get used to it and maybe find some joy and peace in solitude. Try to sit in a coffee shop by yourself. Have a drink or snack. Do not bring your phone or computer. Try to stay comfortable in the solitude and practice being aware of your surroundings and yourself.

Also, we do not want to ignore other major social responsibilities, such as giving back to society. We find the most effective way in which to consistently follow through is to make sure that it is something that logistically fits your schedule and something you hold close to your set of personal values. This could be participating in a political march or volunteering at an animal shelter. You can continually work on changing and refining your social responsibility interests as your life changes.

Health Responsibilities

Health responsibilities include your physical and your mental health. At ages 22/23, you will be choosing your own meals and dedicating yourself to some sort of physical exercise. You will now be responsible for feeding yourself in a healthy manner, which means less junk food than you did in college or your younger years (e.g., pizza, chips, etc.). You can still have these items, but they need to be balanced with an overall healthy diet (e.g., vegetables, fruits, and protein). You must now make doctor's appointments for yourself and follow through (though we hope you have started to make these appointments when you were younger). You will learn what a CBC is, or a "complete blood count." You will now have to learn what your cholesterol levels mean (hint: it comes in four measurements: Total, HDL, LDL, and triglycerides). Did you know that you want a high HDL and a low LDL? HDL is a protective lipoprotein that prevents heart attacks, while LDL does the opposite. It is important to become knowledgeable about what is going on with your own physical health. Personal responsibility is positively correlated with a better physical outcome. It is not the job of your physician to make you healthy, it is their job to guide and provide you with the best choices to choose from.

These principles also apply to your mental health. Twenty-five percent of children up to the age of 18 are either clinically anxious or depressed.[5] These numbers vary with type of disorder throughout adulthood. For those of you with a history of a mental health disorder, we recommend you be extremely proactive in making sure you are on top of your own symptoms and that new ones do not develop. Our rule of thumb is that if you start experiencing more symptoms than not for at least two to three weeks and they are not going away with the skills you have already acquired, it is time to reach out to a mental health professional. Preventing the symptoms from developing into a more severe form is the best, evidence-based approach. We recommend www.abct.org or www.adaa.org and press "Find a therapist" in your area.

Use the following worksheet to assess what you think your specific responsibilities will be at age 22/23. Take into consideration what was discussed in this chapter.

What kind of job (full-time, part-time, what type of job) do you see yourself having?

How much does that job typically give you per week (or month) as a starting/entry position?

Where do you want to live, and do you want to live with roommates?

What is the rent for a room (with roommates) in your desired area (city, country, suburb) vs. alone in a studio/one or two-bedroom?

Will you receive any external financial assistance (e.g., your parents, etc.)?

What do you have to budget for? List them out. For example, (housing/rent, cleaning, food, fun, clothes, health insurance, savings, etc.)?

Recognizing What You Do Not Know

Start thinking about what you can implement in your life now to get you on the track to becoming a successful young adult who operates independently.

You can ask your caregivers/parents/siblings for constructive feedback about what they think of your current repertoire (range) of responsibilities and particularly the ones you struggle with at present. Above, we provided the example of living in New York City at 22/23 years of age. However, you may choose a different path. You may want to work on a farm in Utah, work on a cruise ship, or live in South Carolina in a small town by the beach. The opportunities are endless, which makes this prospect both exciting and scary. If you go on social media and you type in the tag "#dayinthelife" and "#[city/boat/beach]" you can find people who discuss what their daily life consists of (e.g., daily costs), but remember if they have a lot of followers, they may be giving you a glossier version of reality. Look up many examples, but the truth is you will not fully know what your responsibilities will be until you are in it yourself. Use this book as a superpower to prepare you as best you can.

References

1 National Association of Colleges and Employers (NACE). Salary survey report. Bethlehem (PA): NACE; 2026. ISSN 1520-8648.
2 Wittmann M, Lehnhoff S. Age effects in perception of time. *Psychol Rep.* 2005;96(3):741–754.
3 Wittmann M. The inner experience of time. *Philos Trans R Soc B Biol Sci.* 2009;364(1525):1955–1967.
4 Brown T. Gen Z. *Homeownership lags as costs keep it out of reach.* Emarketer; 2026 Jan 28. Available from: https://www.emarketer.com
5 Bitsko RH, Holbrook JR, Ghandour RM, Blumberg SJ, Visser SN, Perou R, et al. Epidemiology and impact of healthcare provider–diagnosed anxiety and depression among US children. *J Dev Behav Pediatr.* 2018;39(5):395–401.

5 Developing Distress Tolerance

Defining Distress Tolerance

Distress tolerance is defined as a person's ability to manage difficult emotions without further worsening the situation.[1] Tolerating high levels of distress and the ability to return to baseline in a safe, effective manner helps with building resilience to face new challenges. Distress tolerance is an important skill to acquire on the age spectrum all the way from infancy to older adulthood. We all need to know how to tolerate our distress ourselves because no one else can jump inside our body and do it for us, as hard as they might try. Dialectical Behavior Therapy (DBT) is a type of evidence-based therapy that has a subcomponent that covers effective processing of difficult emotions, known as *distress tolerance*.[2]

The ability to develop distress tolerance in the face of adverse life events will give you the resilience to endure through those conditions and achieve what you want from life. Distress tolerance skills typically include addressing both the physical and psychological responses to distress. They comprise increasing your awareness of those responses in a non-judgmental manner through a skill called *mindfulness*. This is followed by assessing your current emotional state and then engaging in a coping strategy that best fits what is needed in that moment to cope, both in the short- and long-term.

Tolerating Internal Emotions

As humans, we experience a wide spectrum of emotions—sadness, joy, frustration, fear, etc. When dealing with situations that we perceive as threatening (e.g., meeting new people, giving a presentation, or preparing for college), our brains are wired to activate the flight-or-fight response. The flight-or-fight response is an automatic physiological response to an event that is perceived as stressful and life-threatening. Specifically, the sympathetic nervous system is activated which prepares the body to fight or run.

DOI: 10.4324/9781003649410-5

These physiological responses might include rapid heartbeat, muscle tension, nausea, sweating, hyperventilation, and racing thoughts. As our racing thoughts are trying to evaluate the danger to our lives, we might experience intense emotions that could also be frightening. These frightening thoughts and emotions could themselves become part of the perceived threat and could hinder our ability to tolerate the stressful situation.

Tolerating External Situations

As we notice the push and pull and fight-or-flight feeling inside ourselves when going through a stressful situation, we are faced with the challenge of either tolerating the distress or avoiding it altogether. Our physical responses and racing thoughts can give way to intense emotions. For example, if you are preparing to give a presentation and you begin to experience frightening thoughts like, "What if I say something stupid? What if people laugh at me? What if I stutter?" If these thoughts are then accompanied by emotions such as fear, anxiety, and dread, you might choose to avoid the presentation altogether. If you struggle with tolerating distress and choose to avoid the presentation, this reinforces the likelihood that next time will be just as distressing, if not more. In behavioral science, this is the process of negative reinforcement, and the way anxiety and negative emotions get reinforced and stronger over time.

Recommended Methods of Coping

There are several skills we can learn to cope with distress. Below are specific skills and exercises we encourage you to practice in order to reduce your physical and psychological distress.

Mindfulness

Sometimes people think of mindfulness as sitting still in a meditative state. Mindfulness does not require someone to sit still but *rather* notice their thoughts and emotions in a non-judgmental manner as if you were watching them on a screen. Research has shown that mindfulness skills can be helpful in slowing down one's tendency to impulsively react based on fear and improve attention to the present moment.[3] Let us practice with a couple of mindfulness exercises.

Mindfulness Exercises

Three-Minute Breathing Space[4]

This is a mindfulness exercise that can be done within a few minutes. Once you get a sense of the skills targeted in this practice, you can access them anywhere and at any time. The three steps included in this practice are first attending to what is going on in your body and mind, narrowing your attention to your breath and finally broadening your attention back to your entire body and any sensations that are present.

The following is a three-minute breathing space mindfulness script:[4]

STEPS

1 Whether standing or sitting, change your posture by straightening your back to feel fully engaged.

   a See what is going on in your mind and body right now (e.g., "What thoughts am I thinking or experiencing?")

2 Close your eyes, if possible, or shift your gaze down to one focused spot on the ground (to reduce distractions)

   a Narrow the spotlight of your attention on the sensations of breath in your stomach/abdomen
   b Notice the physical sensations of your breath, as they go in and out
   c If your mind wanders, just make a note (it is not good or bad) and bring your attention back to your breathing

   Note: Deep breathing techniques will be discussed more in detail in Chapter 7.

3 Expanding your focus-take in a deep breath as if your entire body (not just your stomach) is experiencing it and absorbing the oxygen in the air

   a Be aware of your facial expressions
   b Be aware of the feelings or sensations on your face and in your body
   c Notice what your posture is in this moment (make sure to just notice and not judge it as "good or bad")

What did you notice while practicing this exercise?

Note down any thoughts, feelings, and/or sensations

____

____

____

____

Mindful Eating

Have you ever noticed the last time you really savored your favorite treat or drink? If you are like most of us, we are typically busy engaging in multiple tasks and not really noticing this experience. Let us take a moment and take notice of the thoughts, feelings, and sensations associated with this activity.

You may choose whatever food/drink item (candy, raisin, water, tea) and begin practicing with the following script:

Start by noticing how you are feeling right now (tired, calm, weary, surprised, etc.). Then, look at your candy/raisin/tea by holding it in your hand. What colors do you notice? What's the texture look like? Smooth or rough? If your mind wanders to other thoughts, just gently bring it back to noticing the color or texture of the item you are holding in your hand. Next, feel it in your hand. Is it light or heavy? What does the surface feel like? Now, let's engage the sense of smell. Bring it up to your nose and take a deep breath. What does it smell like? Sweet or savory? Let's have you prepare to engage your sense of taste. Take a small sip or bite and let it sit in your mouth. Notice the initial tastes or the way your mouth reacts to the sensation of the eating/drinking. Notice your judgments. Observe but do not judge. Your experience is valid but withhold on saying it is a "good" or "bad." Is the food sweet or sour? Now slowly chew and swallow it. At the same time, notice your thoughts, feelings, and sensations.

What are your notes on slowing down this experience?

____

____

____

____

Try to practice a mindfulness exercise for 3-4x/week to develop the skill of noticing thoughts, feelings, and sensations that serve as a roadblock to you effectively managing distress.

Subjective Units of Distress Assessment

Mindfulness skills are helpful for assessing your current emotional state and intensity. In cognitive-behavioral therapy, a common scale that is used to assess the intensity of distressing emotions is called Subjective Units of Distress scale (SUDs). In some ways, it is like checking your emotional thermometer. Are you cool and calm or are you boiling over with intense emotions? It ranges from "0" (no distress/calm/bored) to "10" (highest level of distress/unbearable emotional suffering). Distressing emotions can include frustration, anger, anxiety, fear, or sadness (Figure 5.1).

Take a moment right now and assess your SUDs using the scale below:

Rate your current SUDS: __________

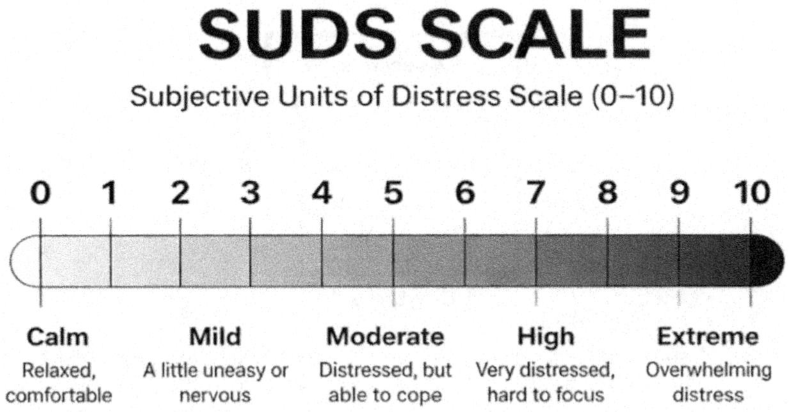

Figure 5.1 A horizontal scale labeled "SUDS Scale: Subjective Units of Distress (0–10)" shows increasing levels of distress from left to right. The scale ranges from 0 (calm, relaxed, comfortable), through mild (a little uneasy or nervous), moderate (distressed but able to cope), and high (very distressed, hard to focus), to 10 (extreme, overwhelming distress).

What was helpful for you to assess the intensity of your current emotions?

____

____

____

____

Did you assess using your thoughts, feelings, or sensations? What did you notice?

____

____

____

____

Paced Breathing

It is commonplace to feel chest pressure or lightheadedness during a state of intense emotions, or if you are engaged in hyperventilation (breathing hard and quickly), which activates your fight-or-flight response. Paced breathing allows us to slow down our breathing and heart rate to help decrease the intensity of our distress[5,6] (Figure 5.2).

Practice by using the box breathing technique. Start by slowly inhaling through your nose, slowly counting to four. Then, hold your breath for

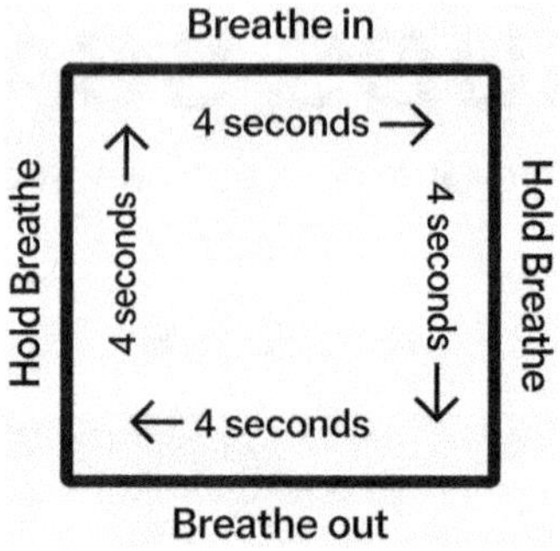

Figure 5.2 A square diagram illustrates a box breathing exercise. Arrows move clockwise with each side labeled "4 seconds": breathe in (top), hold breath (right), breathe out (bottom), and hold breath (left), forming a continuous cycle.

four seconds. Next, slowly exhale through your mouth for four seconds. Repeat this pattern about three more times or until you feel a decrease in your SUDS level.

Progressive Muscle Relaxation[6,7]

For this exercise, you will be targeting the tension in your muscles. You can tense your muscles by section starting with the head, down to your shoulders, through your back and arms, then finally your legs and feet. Between each section of your body (head, upper torso, lower torso, legs/feet), inhale and exhale slowly for five to ten seconds.

For example, start with the head/neck area by lifting your eyebrows and scrunching your nose/mouth for five seconds then release and notice the sensations while slowly inhaling/exhaling for several seconds. After your head, lift your shoulders up to ears while tensing up your arms toward your shoulders and then release after five seconds. Slowly inhale and exhale for several seconds. Now, move toward your back by squeezing your shoulder blades together for five seconds then release. Notice the sensations and slowly breathe in and out. Lastly, focus your lower body area. Tense up your buttocks and lift your legs while flexing up your feet. Hold this position for five seconds then release. Slowly inhale and exhale while noticing the sensations. Notice the tension. Some people find it useful to give the tension a color or consistency, like a hot pink goo, flowing out of your bodily areas into the world around you. This technique is explained again and in more detail in Chapter 7 if you require more practice.

Soothing the Senses[6,7]

Another way of reducing the intensity of your emotions is by *soothing the senses*. We take in a lot of information through our senses and when we are in a flight/fight response state, we might misinterpret the significance of that information.

Make note of activities or things that feel soothing to each of your senses:

Vision: (Examples—watching a favorite show/short video, looking at flower, your favorite color, a picture of your pet-something that is visually pleasing)

___

Hearing: (Examples—listen to music, the sound of rain)

___

Touch: (Examples—wear your favorite sweatshirt, cuddle with a cozy blanket, give someone a hug)

___

Smell: (Examples—light a candle, spritz a soothing scent in the room)

___

Taste: (Examples—eat a cookie, sip on a hot cocoa or favorite tea)

___

Movement: (Examples—stretch your body, take a walk outside, dance)

___

5-4-3-2-1 Grounding Technique

In this exercise, you use the five senses to identify five things you can see around you, four things you can touch, three things you can hear, two things you can smell and one thing you can taste. Complete this technique in repetition over two to three minutes. It is meant to "ground" you so your mind and body can realize it does not need to be in "flight or flight."

Participate in a Competing Activity

Sometimes we might find ourselves feeling stuck in our emotions or having urges to cope in ways that will make the situation worse. It is just at this time when you might find it helpful to engage in an activity that competes with the way your emotions urge you to behave.

For example, if you experience rejection or negative feedback, you might have the urge to disengage by quitting or withdrawing. Maybe you feel angered by the experience, and you might want to yell. In these instances, the best way to cope with these intense emotions without making the situation worse is engaging in a competing response that is opposite to your urges. If you want to yell, instead go exercise or go for a walk. Or, if your reaction to a scary meeting with your supervisor at work is to avoid going to work, a competing response would be to attend work and proactively go and find your supervisor. Oftentimes, the anticipation of a distressing event is far worse than the actual experience.

Challenge Your Thinking

A strategy that helps working toward facing a fear is challenging your thought processes. When experiencing distressing emotions, your ability to process thoughts is negatively affected by your misinterpretation of a perceived threat. A type of cognitive-behavioral strategy (evidence-based) called cognitive restructuring works to challenge your misinterpretations and extreme thinking to more accurately arrive at a solution that is the best response for your situation.[7] We will go into more detail on this in Chapter 7.

Case Example

Sarah is a 17-year-old junior in high school who is preparing to take her SATs and has several colleges in mind that she would like to apply for next year. She feels very anxious about obtaining a good SAT score and is experiencing significant doubt about her ability to get a high enough score for her preferred colleges. She feels that if she does not get that high score, she will be rejected by *all* the colleges she applies to next year.

Here is how Sarah might challenge her distressing thoughts:

Situation: I'm taking my SAT's next weekend for college applications in the fall.

Distressing Thoughts: "If I don't get a high score, then I won't get into my top college, and I will be a failure. What if all the colleges I applied to reject me!"

Emotions and SUDS rating: Anxiety—7.

Challenging the thoughts: (What are the facts of the situation? What's the evidence for/against?): Well, this is the first time I'm taking the SATs and I'm allowed to take it again later. My college counselor shared with us that colleges also consider all my academic experiences including that I'm captain of the volleyball team and treasurer of the student council. Those activities count too!

Emotions and SUDs rating after countering the distressing thought: Anxiety—3.

Practice

Now try it for your own situation:
Situation:

____

____

____

Emotion and SUDs rating:

____

____

Challenging your thoughts: (What are the facts? What's the evidence? What's the worst that can happen? Can I cope with it?)

____

____

Emotion and SUDs rating after:

____

____

Each of the skills mentioned above has you moving toward the stressor by managing distress vs. engaging in avoidance behaviors. When we move toward the stressor by effectively managing distress, we build confidence in our ability to cope with similar situations. If we engage in avoidance, then you can rob yourself from the chance of learning and growing from the experience. You want to build resilience and learn how to master adapting to setbacks through acceptance of your thoughts, emotions, and the situation.

Acceptance

Even our best efforts to manage our distress and work though challenging situations will not always get us to our desired outcome. This is where practicing skills of acceptance may help us persevere in the face of challenges and become resilient. To be clear, acceptance is not approval of the undesired situation or passivity in the face of adversity. Acceptance is also not a goal, but rather a process.

According to Dr. Russ Harris, acceptance is about actively accepting distressing thoughts, feelings, memories, and taking action to cope with the situation.[8] According to Linehan, acceptance is when we stop struggling with reality and live a fulfilling life even when painful events occur.[1] In other words, we should aim to accept our distress and tolerate it enough to continue to live a productive and fruitful life.

One way to practice acceptance is through self-compassion. Engaging in self-compassion will help you let go of the inner struggle to fight against the reality of an unwanted situation. It is not necessarily giving yourself reassurance. It is telling yourself, given the distressing situation, it makes sense, and it is ok that you are reacting in a certain way. You are validating your reaction to the experience, which will allow you to open fully and engage in identifying a strategy to work through it.

In summary, intense emotions in reaction to difficult situations are a normal part of the human experience and do not have to interfere with or halt progress in our life. By practicing the skills in this chapter, you will be better able to tolerate the challenges associated with life transitions as an upcoming young adult.

Below we have included a weekly checklist of skills for you to practice.

Worksheet to Practice Distress Tolerance

For the next week, make time each day to practice at least one or two of the following skills:

Distress tolerance skill	*Day 1 (SUDs before/ after)*	*Day 2 (SUDs before/ after)*	*Day 3 (SUDs before/ after)*	*Day 4 (SUDs before/ after)*	*Day 5 (SUDs before/ after)*	*Day 6 and 7 (weekends) (SUDs before/after)*	*Day 5 (SUDs before/ after)*	*Day 6/7 (SUDs before/ after)*
Mindfulness exercise: ________								
Paced breathing								
Progressive muscle relaxation								
Soothe the senses								
Engaging in a competing response: ________								
Challenge your thinking								
Problem-solving								
Acceptance								

1) Did you notice changes in your SUDs level after each skill practice? Did you find one set of skills that worked best for you?

____

____

____

____

2) Make note of the distress tolerance skills that worked the best for you and build your distress tolerance tool kit below:

____

____

____

____

I'd like to include the following in my toolkit:

____

____

____

____

References

1 Linehan MM. *DBT skills training manual.* 2nd ed. New York (NY): Guilford Press; 2015.
2 Linehan MM, Armstrong HE, Suarez A, Allmon D, Heard HL. Cognitive-behavioral treatment of chronically parasuicidal borderline patients. *Arch Gen Psychiatry.* 1991;48(12):1060–1064.
3 Chiesa A, Calati R, Serretti A. Does mindfulness training improve cognitive abilities? A systematic review of neuropsychological findings. *Clin Psychol Rev.* 2011;31(3):449–464.
4 Williams M, Penman D. *Mindfulness: an eight-week plan for finding peace in a frantic world.* London: Piatkus; 2011.
5 Toussaint L, Nguyen Q, Roettger C, Dixon K, Offenbacher M, Kohls N, et al. Randomized trial showing progressive muscle relaxation and deep breathing increased psychological and physiological relaxation compared to control. *Evid Based Complement Alternat Med.* 2021;2021:1–2.
6 Wright K. Box breathing: a tool for stress management. *J Nurs Educ Pract.* 2017;7(3):90–93.
7 Beck AT. *Cognitive therapy and emotional disorders.* New York (NY): International Universities Press; 1976.
8 Harris R. *ACT made simple: an easy-to-read primer on acceptance and commitment therapy.* 2nd ed. Oakland (CA): New Harbinger Publications; 2019.

6 Managing Your Social Connections and Expectations

In this chapter, we will discuss the importance of social connections in our daily lives as we move from high school through early adulthood (22/23 years of age). We start the chapter by exploring who is in our social support group. Then, we discuss how that social support network can change over time depending on our location, interests, and the amount of energy we have to invest in relationships. Next, we discuss managing our expectations of a wide variety of relationships within these social connections. Finally, we briefly explore some research in the areas of social connection and friendships.

Define Your Social Support Group

Think about who the people in your life are and how they support you. If you wanted to go out to the movies on Saturday night, who would you ask? If you needed help understanding a science assignment, who would be that person? If your car broke down on the highway on a rainy night, who would you call? The benefits of having an adequate social support network have been found repeatedly to be a significant protective factor against both psychological and physiological stress, including depression, burnout, and inflammation.[1–3] Ideally, you would have a wide variety of people in your life to support you with everything from emotional stressors (e.g., coping with a relationship breakup) to practical dilemmas (e.g., help move to a new apartment). Over the past several years, fostering a support system has been increasingly challenging. In fact, the U.S. Surgeon General in 2023 declared loneliness and isolation a public health epidemic.[4] According to the U.S. Surgeon General's Advisory,[4] "far too many Americans lack social connection leading to poor health and negative outcomes."

Within a social support network, it is typical to have a wide range of people who support you to a varying degree. Who we have in our support

DOI: 10.4324/9781003649410-6

network will change as we progress from childhood to adulthood. As young children, the first support people are our family, including parents, siblings, grandparents, members of our extended family, and possibly our teachers.

When we enter school, the kids we meet in school become part of our support system ranging from acquaintances to best friends. This is our first introduction to relationships outside of our families, and we learn to form close bonds with peers who have similar interests to us. Acquaintances are those peers we see in our classes and with whom we are friendly in a superficial manner (e.g., "Hey, how's it going?"). We do not spend time with these classmates socializing outside of class and do not generally share any deeper interests. Close friendships, or best friends, are those who share many similar interests with us, and we feel comfortable being emotionally vulnerable to them. We spend a significant amount of time with these friends across many settings.

As we transition into adolescence, we start to experience romantic relationships. A romantic partner might become a significant source of support. We typically share similar interests with romantic partners and spend a lot of time with each other, possibly more than our platonic best friends.

Those who provide us with mentorship, such as teachers, coaches, and supervisors, are another source of support. At work and school, these relationships can help us navigate challenges as we develop and refine our skills. Teachers who are more supportive and engaged in the classroom generate students with a higher level of positively expressed emotion and academic engagement.[5] Have you experienced a great teacher who was truly interested in your talents? Have you also experienced the opposite? A "bad" teacher? Think about what qualities those teachers had that made them mean something to you, whether positive or negative.

It would be great for a teacher, sports coach, or work supervisor to initiate guidance and mentorship, but it is often necessary for the younger person to engage in effective help-seeking to begin to develop a supportive relationship. In other words, relationships are not one-sided, especially as you get older. It has been found that when students engage in instrumental help seeking (e.g., asking for explanations, feedback), they are more successful learners than students who avoid asking for help.[6] This is also the case when we are interacting with supervisors in the work environment. Employees who engage in adaptive help seeking behaviors that focus on task clarity and skill development are more likely to learn faster, develop more collaborative and respectful work relationships, thus improving work performance.[6] Feeling comfortable with initiating support (being the first to try) in your relationships, and nurturing relationships with teachers and supervisors will often lead to success across the school and work environment.

How Do Your Social Relationships Change?

Do you remember how you were able to make friends as a small child at a playground? It was relatively easy, and it probably went something like this, "Do you want to play?" and there you had an instant friend! As we grow older and our interests change, making and keeping friends is more challenging. When we transition into middle school through high school, we notice peers getting together around activities and interests such as sports, video games, and theater. We even notice peers start identifying with these groups such as the sports-oriented peers, science/tech-oriented peers or drama club kids. We may even see ourselves throughout middle school and high school switching from one group to the other as the focus of our primary interests change. You can also fit in with many groups as opposed to just one.

As you move from high school to college, your social relationships will naturally change. In high school, friendships often revolve around shared activities, classes, and daily routines, making them feel stable and familiar. However, in college, your social circle may shift as you meet new people with diverse backgrounds, interests, and values. Some high school friendships will remain strong, while others may fade as you and your friends grow in different directions. A major difference in relationship development between high school and college is the amount of time spent with friends engaging in daily activities. In college, you may attend many of the same classes as your roommates or students living on the same dorm floor. You may have several meals a week with them and study together. Additionally, you may engage in fun activities together such as attending concerts or parties. The amount of time we spend together on fun and leisure activities predicts how close we feel in our friendships with others. Research on friendship development has found that it can take over 200 hours to move from *friend* to *best friend.7*

Young adulthood during post-college years (22/23 years of age) offers its own potential challenges for developing and supporting friendships as you move from being a student to living independently and taking part in the workforce. You may find that it is more difficult to gather with peers around similar interests given a more structured work schedule only allows for social activities early in the morning or later in the evening after work. You may find that it takes more effort to get to know others to the same level as you did when you were in college. You must make more of an effort to increase social connections by signing up for social activities such as a recreational sports team, book club, or community volunteering to increase contact with those who share the same interests. This is an opportunity to reflect on both the quality and quantity of those in your closest social circle as you look to balance work obligations with social connections that meet your personal needs. If you are a person who identifies as an introvert, you likely prefer to have a smaller circle of friends who share similar social activities and interests, such as reading and conversation. If you are an extrovert, you likely enjoy being with a larger group of friends, going to concerts, dance clubs, or taking part in sports or team recreational activities. If you are the latter, you might enjoy a larger amount of people in your social network who are readily available to get together for activities.

Who we have in our social support network will change over time to adapt to our own social and emotional developmental stage in life. Developing friendships at school as a teen will vary from developing friendships once you are an adult. Let us go over how to create social connections at these different life stages, as it takes a different set of skills to adapt.

Developing Social Support Groups at Different Life Stages (and Ages)

High School (Secondary School) Years

Given the structure that is generally available to you in high school, developing and keeping a support group often starts with shared activities—sports teams, clubs, study groups, or even online communities. You are generally interacting with peers every day during structured activities such as attending classes and school-organized social events. At this stage, friendships typically form through regular interactions in the school environment, which eases seeking out peers who share your values and interests. As a teen, it is expected that your interests may change over time as you learn about what you value the most. Thus, it is important to be open to creating a wider network of friends. Maybe at this stage you have close friends who you have known since kindergarten and feel comfortable. At the same time, it is good practice to expand friendships with other groups who also share your interests. As you and your friends transition to the college years, the ability to interact with a wide range of social groups will make it easier for you to develop friendships in that new social environment.[8]

College/University Years

College is typically the first time most young adults cohabit (live in the same dwellings) with peers. In this social situation, there is a significant level of proximity where you share classes, eat meals, and live together. According to Dr. Hall, the mere number of hours spent together can help build social connections, though simply attending classes and eating at the same dining hall will not automatically result in developing close friendships.[7] According to Dr. Hall's research, engaging in nonobligatory social activities together helps with fostering social connections more than engaging in work-oriented tasks.[7] Unlike high school, friendships may require more effort to develop and support despite having more frequent contact with peers. Other research has shown that there are opportunities during a college student's experience in which it is better to find a friend. In her research, Dr. McCabe showed that there are "friendship markets" during certain times in the academic year in which students are open to developing new friendships.8 These times include the start of the freshman year when there are student orientation activities, and everyone is new to the environment as they explore what the campus has to offer. These "friendship market" opportunities also exist for other college years in which students are returning to campus and open to exploring new social opportunities. As a college student, it might mean you will have to expand your social network wider and take part in several activities on campus, such as playing a sport or participating in a structured social group such as fraternity/sorority. At the same time, it is also valuable for college students to find mentors as part of their social support system, whether professors, advisors, or older students, who can provide guidance during this transition. Developing a reliable support system in college fosters emotional well-being and helps with academic and personal challenges. The experience and practice of developing a social support network that includes close friends and mentors will help with knowing how to foster these same connections in your post-college adult life.

22/23 Years of Age and Beyond

After college, forming and supporting social connections requires intentional effort, hard work, and patience. Without the built-in structure of school, friendships often stem from work, hobbies, or community activities. The added responsibilities that come from post-college/trade school adult life further complicate finding time and energy to invest in social connections. For young adults in their post-education life, this might be the first exposure to the typical five days per week/ eight hours plus per day work schedule. Many might even have jobs that require more than 40 hours per week. On top of that, you likely moved to a different city for your first professional job. Developing social connections is more challenging but not impossible if you are not actively engaged and have patience with the process. As discussed previously, increasing social contact with peers includes proximity and hours of engaging in activities centered around mutual interests.[3,7] This would include joining professional organizations that meet regularly for networking, volunteering at a nonprofit, or engaging in community social events. Unlike your high school and college years, friendships in adulthood often revolve around shared values and mutual support rather than convenience. Although you will have added responsibility for work and managing adult responsibilities, prioritizing meaningful relationships and supporting regular communication through scheduling meet ups or checking in via text/phone call will be beneficial to your overall well-being.

As you continue through adulthood, your responsibilities will continue to grow and expand to take up more of your time and energy. This will also be the case for those in your social support network as they may develop long-term romantic relationships and social priorities begin to shift. For other stages of adulthood, meaningful friendships and other social support are still important and worth investing time in supporting these connections. As with earlier stages of your life, developing relationships with others centered around shared interests and values can still happen—keeping in mind proximity (neighbors, coworkers, fellow parents at your child's school) and number of hours spent fostering those relationships. Getting on a group text of social connections is a great starting point, but fostering those relationships through check-ins and active participation is vital in creating more close relationships.

Worksheet—Interests and Hobbies that Can Foster Connections with Others

For this exercise, take a moment to think about the social groups in your school or community and how they are a match to your personal interests. Below (column on the left), circle interests and hobbies you *currently* engage in. Circle the ones you participate in, not hope to take part in. In the other column (to the right), circle social groups in your community or school that you take part in and put a star next to those that you would like to be a part of or join.

Personal interests/hobbies	*Actual social groups joined (or to join)*
Playing on sports teams	Religious youth group
Dancing	School/town sports team
Playing musical instruments	Marching band
Creative writing	Outdoor or ski club
Physical activity (running, etc.)	Anime club
Being out in nature, camping	Cheer team
Video games	Board game club (e.g., D&D)
Board games	Scouts
Crafts, drawing	Volunteering at a food bank
Caring for animals	Volunteering at an animal shelter
Baking and cooking	Joining a school or community theater group
Social justice	Participating in a march/protest
Spirituality/religion	Youth groups
More: ________________	________________
More: ________________	________________

Social Connections and Technology

Technology, including social media and chat rooms, can help to foster social connections with others who have similar interests and hobbies. In fact, some interests and hobbies are facilitated using technology such as online role-playing games (RPGs). If you have an interest in social causes, you might connect with a local community through their social media account. However, technology should not be a substitute for in-person social connections in your community. Reciprocal relationships must be supported via regular meaningful interactions that would include texting, video call, and meeting up in-person. If your social interactions are limited to the online world, you will miss out on subtle social nonverbal communication that can inform you about the relationship. If you find that your social connections are limited to online, take steps to reduce your use of social technologies and engage with in-person get-togethers. Research shows that individuals who passively engage in social technology through passive scrolling with no direct communication report feeling lonelier and more isolated than those who use it to actively enhance their in-person social connections.[9] It is also *very* important if you are under the age of 18 to ask your guardian's permission to engage in these activities and to have them be supervised. As bullying can occur without the knowledge of your support system, make sure to make others aware of how you are trying to establish social connections for your own safety.

Managing Your Expectations and Putting in the Hard Work

Friendships can flourish in various places, but require some key ingredients to develop and maintain. We must consider where relationships fit in our lives and the degree to which we feel emotionally invested in a particular relationship. Whether we socialize at work or in the community (e.g., gym, volunteer work), sociologists have found that proximity, shared interests, and vulnerability are the main drivers to developing and supporting a variety of friendships. Friendships can take the form of acquaintance, casual friend, friend, and close friend.[3] Each one provides an important social support function depending on what is needed at the moment. Acquaintances are people who you see in class or at work, and you know their name, but you do not share any detailed personal information with them. They might have a sense of your routine such as attending a class at a certain time or that you take the train to work, but nothing beyond polite "small talk." A casual friend is someone you have moved past typical "small talk" and occasionally have contact outside of the settings where you have met. You might exchange quick text messages with each other or grab a coffee with them between classes. They are likely someone you contact if you have a question about a class assignment, but not a friend you typically contact during a personal crisis.

A "friend" is someone with whom you will have shared reciprocal (goes both ways) emotional and intimate information as part of your relationship. Per Dr. Hall, you will likely have spent 80–100 hours interacting with them outside of formal, structured settings (e.g., class, work).3 In fact, you likely have interacted with this friend in a wide variety of environments such as working out together at the gym, attending concerts, and/or socializing in their homes. Finally, we have friendships with whom we spent meaningful time within a variety of activities of shared interests and values who we refer to as a close friend ("best friend"). According to Hall, these types of close connections require 200+ hours of social time, where you get to know each other's values, social history, vulnerabilities, and long-term goals.[3,7] These are the first friends you call when you are in crisis.

Not every person you meet in your classes or at work will be a friend. They might stay at the acquaintance level; a friendly face when you enter the classroom or your office. Furthermore, not every friend will move onto being a close friend, especially if there is a lack of proximity, shared interests/values or meaningful activities to connect. Even if there is one of those three ingredients, the other two must also be present to foster a closer connection. For example, a dorm roommate has the potential to become a close friend, but if you do not have shared interests or values and do not engage in meaningful activities other than a shared living space then that relationship will not likely turn into a close friendship.

Further, not every relationship you have (whether romantic, friendship, or even family) may be what you would like it to be (e.g., quality, time spent). It is important to recognize not every person who wants to fit with you will and not every person you want to match with you, will (in any form of a relationship). Many times, it has absolutely nothing to do with you (just like not every key fits every lock). However, sometimes, you will need to self-reflect to examine your contribution to the relationship.

Worksheet—Are You Setting Aside Time for Connecting with Others?

Now that you have information about what kind of investment it takes to develop diverse types of relationships, reflect on the closeness of your current social connections. Use the form below and list your current peer social connections and their friendship category. Select three social relationships that you would like to focus on to develop a closer relationship. Using the information from this section, be realistic with the proximity, time and energy you must invest in each relationship. When identifying hours, keep in mind that you want those hours to be mostly leisure, nonobligatory hours within the past six months. For example, if you have an acquaintance in your SAT prep tutoring class, a two-hour per week class, that time should not be counted toward the friendship time. Finally, name an action plan for each friendship to take it to the level you prefer.

Name	*Current est. hours*	*Current friendship category*	*Goal category*	*Hours needed*	*Action plan*
Example: Jane	15 hours	Acquaintance—classmate	Casual friend	35 more hours	Invite me for a coffee or lunch between classes

Research on the Effect of Social Connections in Building Relationships

Thus far, we have discussed the importance of building a social connection in various stages of life and strategies to foster different levels of friendships within those connections. Social connections give us a sense of belonging through the presence of social bonds. The benefits are also experienced on a biological level. Reciprocal social connections lower cortisol and reduce stress on the body.[10]

Having frequent social connections, which include contact with people within your proximity, is not enough to form meaningful relationships. According to research on young adult friendships, we can have social connections without many friends if you have mostly "weak ties" (which consist of frequent, pleasant interactions with acquaintances).[3,7] In young adulthood, the goal is to use social connections to build a "friendship network" of various levels of closeness that support your life.7 As mentioned in the earlier sections of this chapter, the steps needed to develop a network of acquaintances, friends, and close friends takes investment and time from each of us. Social connections are vital in protecting us from psychological and physiological stress.

References

1 Adam EK, et al. Day-to-day dynamics of social interactions and cortisol: evidence for a role of loneliness and social support. *J Pers Soc Psychol*. 2006;90(1):1–20.
2 Choi KW, et al. An exposure-wide and Mendelian randomization approach to identifying modifiable factors for the prevention of depression. *Am J Psychiatry*. 2020;177(10):944–954.

3 Hall JA. How many hours does it take to make a friend? *J Soc Pers Relat*. 2019;36(4):1278–1296.
4 Hall JA, Merolla AJ. *The social biome: how everyday communication connects and shapes us*. New Haven (CT): Yale University Press; 2025.
5 Kennedy E. A study of students' fears of seeking academic help from teachers. *J Classr Interact*. 1997;32(1):11–17.
6 McCabe JM. *Making, keeping, and losing friends: how campuses shape college students' networks*. Chicago (IL): University of Chicago Press; 2025.
7 Orben A, Przybylski AK. The association between adolescent well-being and digital technology use: A large-scale study. *Nat Hum Behav*. 2019;3:173–182.
8 Roorda DL, et al. The influence of affective teacher–student relationships on students' school engagement and achievement: a meta-analytic approach. *Rev Educ Res*. 2011;81(4):493–529.
9 U.S. Department of Health and Human Services. *Our epidemic of loneliness and isolation: the U.S. Surgeon General's advisory on the healing effects of social connection and community*. Washington (DC): Office of the Surgeon General; 2023.
10 Yang YC, et al. Social relationships and physiological determinants of longevity across the human life span. *Proc Natl Acad Sci U S A*. 2016;113(3):578–583.

7 Problem-Solving and Opportunities for "Successful Failures"

How Do We Define Problem-Solving?

In your elementary school years, solving a "problem" equates to a simple question that needs to be answered. For example, "what do you want for lunch?" As you get older, problems become more complex. What classes will I take in high school? What do I want to do after high school? College? Trade school?

The first step in solving a problem is to identify the largest problem that you need to address. Second, make a flow chart that identifies several smaller/sub-problems under the main problem. For example, see the chart below (Figure 7.1):

As seen above, under the header of the "large" problem ("where do I attend college?"), there are several sub-factors/sub-problems to consider. There is no one right answer to these questions; all of us will have our own individual preference. Some of us might choose a larger class, while some a smaller one. One person may care about attending a school with Division I sports, but another person may not care. At this stage of life, it is also hard to consider your own interests and not that of your friend/family/support group. Deciding what you and you alone want can lead to a lot of anxiety, sadness, and worry. It can also lead to a lot of thoughts of uncertainty (e.g., "Did I make the right decision? What is the *right* decision?"), and we want you to recognize that this is not only expected, but what happens to everyone. By their nature, problems that fall into the "large problem" category are the most difficult to solve.

When making these types of complicated and difficult decisions, it is important that you regulate your emotions. As humans, it is *not* possible, nor a goal to be emotionless. However, it is important that strong emotions do not make decisions for us. There needs to be a balance between logic and emotions.

DOI: 10.4324/9781003649410-7

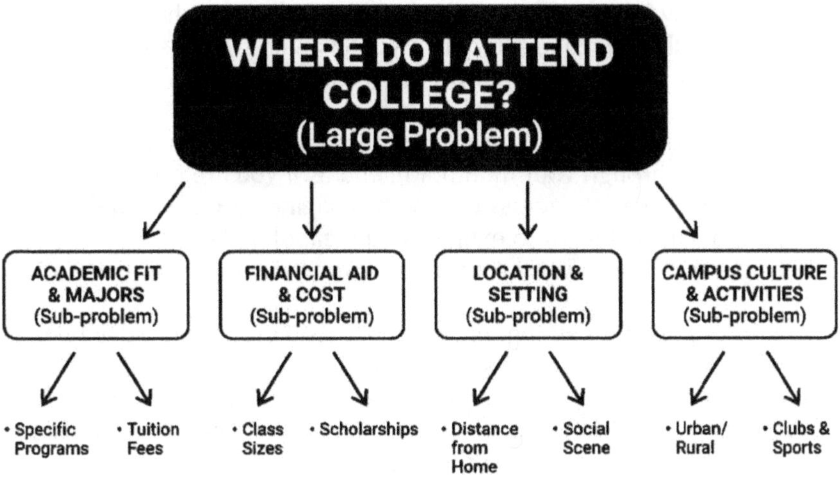

Figure 7.1 A flowchart titled "Where do I attend college? (Large Problem)" breaks the decision into four sub-problems: academic fit and majors, financial aid and cost, location and setting, and campus culture and activities. Each sub-problem includes examples: programs and tuition fees; class sizes and scholarships; distance from home and social scene; and urban or rural setting and clubs or sports.

Coping Mechanisms to Assist in Regulating Your Emotions

Diaphragmatic Breathing (Deep Breathing)

Diaphragmatic breathing, or breathing from the belly, helps to regulate the nervous system and reduce the fight-or-flight response. Deep breathing helps to activate the *para*sympathetic nervous system responsible for a rest and reset response in our body. Remember that the deep breathing technique is not about getting more air and oxygen into your body but more regulating it. Breaths should not be too large, but also not too small. They need to be right in the middle, rhythmed, and paced.

Here are step-by-step instructions on how to complete diaphragmatic/deep breathing:

1 Sit in a comfortable chair (or lay on the ground-whatever is most comfortable for you) with your legs touching the floor and your back upright to the chair's back (or flat on the ground).
2 Place one hand on your belly and the other down your side.

3 Let your body weight relax into the floor or chair. Do not hold yourself up.
4 Take a breath and make sure when you take air in, you stick your belly out, and your hand moves outwards.
5 On your next breath, only take air in with your nose. Make sure the breath is two seconds (say, "one, one thousand, two one thousand").
6 Exhale only through your mouth. Pretend as if you are pursing your lips to blow out a candle across the room. Imagine you are tunneling your breath to narrow the air to extinguish the candle's flame.
7 Repeat this process over the course of three to five minutes (Figure 7.2).

In addition to deep breathing, progressive muscle relaxation also helps to reduce overwhelming emotions and stress.

To quote the character *Ian* in the movie Jurassic Park, "life finds a way." When we experience stress, anxiety, or depression, it finds a way to express itself in our body. For young adults it is common to experience stress as headaches and/or stomachaches. For older adults, many can experience it as muscle pain or back pain. If you were to scan your body like packages are scanned at the grocery store, you would find locations where you store more physical tension.

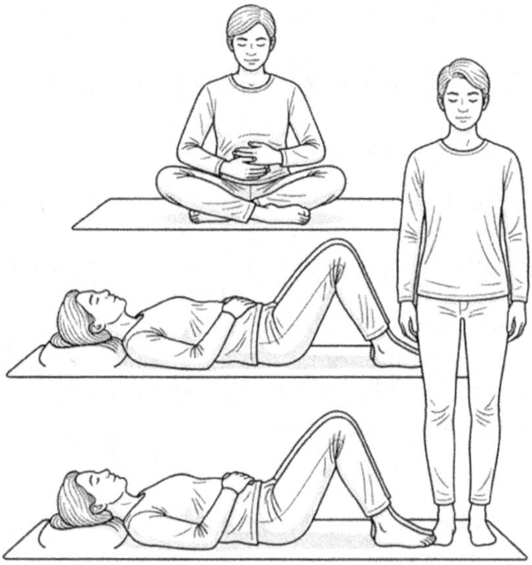

Figure 7.2 A drawing shows a person practicing relaxation in three positions: sitting cross-legged with hands on the abdomen, lying on their back with knees bent and hands on the abdomen, and standing upright with eyes closed. The images suggest focusing on breathing and body awareness in different postures.

Progressive Muscle Relaxation

First, scan your body for tension. Start with your head, move to your temples, then down to your jaw. Examine your neck, shoulders, stomach, legs, feet, and then toes. When you notice areas of tension, focus mainly on these areas. However, if you have the time and a quiet, undisturbed environment you can do the entire program.

Squeeze and tense an area of your body you feel the most tension. Hold that feeling as hard as you can for 15–20 seconds. When you stop tensing, let yourself relax into the new feeling and imagine the tension leaving your body. Some individuals like to imagine their stress/tension as a certain color in their body (e.g., a hot red or pink, we also discussed this as "hot pink goo" two chapters ago) and then imagine that stress leaving your body (e.g., like lava flowing out through the toes and fingertips). Move down from the top of your body to the bottom, as instructed above, and repeat these steps. In total, the process should take you around 15–20 minutes to complete. Any less and you will not gain the benefit, and anymore and you might fall asleep! (Figure 7.3)

Figure 7.3 A four-step illustration demonstrates progressive muscle relaxation. A person sits cross-legged and is instructed to tense the muscles in their arm and shoulder, then hold the tension by clenching a fist. Next, they release and relax the muscles, and finally lie down, noticing the difference as their body fully relaxes.

Restructuring Your Stressful Thoughts

Cognitive restructuring was founded by the psychiatrist Aaron Beck in the 1970s.[1] He found he was experiencing automatic thoughts that were sometimes unhelpful and caused uncomfortable emotions. Therefore, he examined how to challenge the thought process by looking for evidence that a thought was true vs. untrue, a process he labeled *cognitive restructuring*. Cognitive restructuring encourages us to question the validity of our thoughts when they cause us to feel badly about ourselves. There are certain thoughts that we all have, in different forms, that are called *cognitive distortions* (or unhelpful thoughts). Below is a list provided by David Burns.[2] Read over the list below to see if you have any of these types of thoughts. Remember we all have at least some of them, but when they are too strong and/or too frequent that leads us to problems, such as anxiety or depression. If you do identify with the types of thinking below, do not just think of the opposite thought as that will not be helpful. Try to think of your thoughts as a scientist would. What is the evidence for and against them?

Identifying Cognitive Distortions (Unhelpful Ways of Thinking)

- All-or-nothing thinking: Thinking in extreme, absolute ways, right or wrong and nothing in between. Everything is either all black or all white; all good or all bad.
- Overgeneralization: Making conclusions or generalizations from a single event to a larger one. If something bad happens, then it will happen every single time in a similar scenario.
- Mental Filter: Only focusing on negative things while filtering out the positive.
- Discounting the Positive: explaining away positive things and insisting they do not count.
- Jumping to conclusions comes in two forms: *Mind Reading and Fortune Telling*. The former is thinking you know what others are thinking when you do not and the latter is predicting a negative outcome when there is no evidence for it.
- Catastrophizing: Thinking of the worst possible case scenario for yourself. Beginning sentences with the words, "What if…?"
  Emotional Reasoning: If I feel it, then it must be true. "I feel bad; therefore I am bad."
- "Should" statements: Using words such as, I "should," "must," or "have to's," which only serve to make you feel worse about yourself.
- Labeling: Calling yourself negative labels. You may make one mistake in your entire identity.

- Personalization: Finding fault in yourself for something or someone you are not responsible for in the first place.

If you have had any of these thoughts, which are a very common experience among us all, you may need to challenge them if they are happening too frequently and/or are so severe you cannot seem to let them go.

Let's say you are thinking, "what if I never get into college, what if I never get a job?" This type of thinking falls into the *catastrophizing* category. At first, you may feel anxious because of having this thought. However, you need to challenge it by asking yourself, "do I get bad grades? Am I not motivated? Is there any evidence toward thinking I will not go to college?" When you discover there is no evidence to support your fear and that it is just a fear, you start *feeling* better.

Try and use the following example in the following worksheet. We want this to be specific to the age of 22/23 and the stressors and thoughts you may be experiencing then.

The Scenario

You started working at your first job and you ask your boss for feedback on a memo you wrote. Your boss says to you, "I am not your English professor; it is not my job to edit your writing. I am sure what you have is fine; just send it."

What thoughts might you have from this encounter? Fill the worksheet out below (all columns) answering this question. Then, move to the second line and additionally fill out one of your own unhelpful thoughts you may have recently had. Make sure to fill out all the columns and to try and challenge the thought.

Try the worksheet below to practice

Record thought (include time of day, what you were doing)	*Rate emotions and 1–100% and how much you feel them (must equal 100%)*	*Is this a helpful thought? Yes or No?*	*Counter the thought (look at the evidence for and against)*	*Rate emotions How much do you feel them?*
Example: *"I am a bad student because I got an "F" on a test"*	*Scared (10%), frustrated (15%) disappointed (10%), down (10%), anxious (55%)*	*No*	*Examining the evidence*	*Scared-5%, frustration 0%, disappointment-5%, down/sad-0%, anxious, 20%*

Example above:

Your own example:

It is important to try and regulate your thoughts and emotions using the skills above. Then, make attempts to think through how to break your larger problem down into smaller, more manageable parts/problems. You do not need to be all inclusive, but you need to include at least three to four sub-problems that you will likely confront. Use the problems that come into your mind or ask a family member or trusted friend to help you brainstorm.

After you have broken your larger problem down into smaller, more manageable pieces, you can now develop a plan for more proactive action. Look at your calendar and determine if there is a schedule that can be set for you to follow through on each subtask/problem. Phone calendars are great, as you can set noisy alarms/reminders about completing your specific subtask/problem. Second, develop a system to hold yourself accountable. The best way to behaviorally manage and increase your chances of following through is to have a system of accountability in place. Either reward yourself (e.g., shopping) or take something away from yourself (e.g., not watching your favorite show) until the task is complete. You can also ask someone else to hold you accountable (i.e., ask if you have completed the task). Try the steps to completing the subtask on your own first. You also need to be flexible with yourself. You may discover you took on too much or more than you could handle. You may then need to make subtasks for your subtasks. Be willing to be accountable, make mistakes, be flexible, and not give up in this process.

Based on the Steps We Have Discussed, Write out How You May Go about Solving the Following Problem

> You receive a test back from a teacher and notice they marked an item incorrect. You do not notice this until later in the night, after school has finished. You are debating whether to approach the teacher, for fear they think you purposefully changed the answer.

Cheat Sheet of Steps Provided

1 Identify the problem

 Identify sub-problems

2 Identify ways to cope with emotions associated with the problems

 A Which coping mechanism are you using? (e.g., deep breathing, thought challenging, etc.?)

3 Break down the problem into manageable pieces (e.g., keeping to a schedule, accountability, making appointments, seeking out appropriate sources).

A large component to identifying the larger and smaller components of a program is estimating a realistic timeframe. As we get older, life experience teaches us that we need to provide ample time, or 1.5X of the original plan. The reasoning behind this overpreparation is the unpredictability of life and what it throws at us. For example, let us say you are on the way to a dentist appointment at 1pm, but you encounter a car accident on the way. Your arrival time is now 10–15 minutes behind your initial estimate. However, if you have given yourself extra time, you would still arrive five to ten minutes early. Time management plays a rather large role in problem identification and solving.

As you work on giving yourself ample time to complete your task, level of accountability is also essential. Would you be more accountable to finishing the task by yourself or do you need someone else to hold your "feet to the fire?" Are you someone who can follow through on your own, or do you need self-imposed or external consequences? For example, a teacher giving you a deadline is an external consequence. An internal (self) deadline would be finishing a project earlier than due and using a reward (e.g., shopping spree for an afternoon) to follow through to completion. To understand where you fall along the lines of external vs. internal accountability, you need to do a lot of trial-and-error activities (such as below). There is no one right way to operate, but you should gain insight into how you specifically operate as soon as you can. Trust us, it will make life a lot easier for you in the short and long-term.

Example of a Problem You Might Encounter When You Are 22/23 Years Old

Overall/Larger Problem: Applying and getting an *offer* for a full-time job
Smaller Sub/Problems: How much money do you want to make, and what location do you want to live in? Will you have the support of your friends and family?

Week 1

Monday–Wednesday—Answer what areas of the country you want to live in? Then, address these subtasks/problems: cost of living, quality of life, general interests.

Thursday–Saturday—How much money does it require for you to live in these different areas and will you have a support system in each of these locations? Who would that be?

Sunday—Take a break.

Week 2

Monday–Wednesday—Look at your locations and look at different job applications on monster.com, Glassdoor.com and indeed.com

Thursday–Saturday—What do applications require? Does it require working on a resume/CV and should you email your contacts? Do you have those chosen?

Sunday—Take a break.

Week 3

Monday–Wednesday—How many applications will you need to send in? Is there a difference based on the area of the country you are living in?

Thursday–Saturday—Continue researching- are you not thinking of any decisions you need to make?

Sunday—Take a break.

Week 4

Monday–Wednesday—If you get a job interview, how will you prepare?

Thursday–Friday—Examine questions for preparation? What to wear? Do you need a mock interview? Will you have familiarized yourself with the job description and mission of the company?

Saturday/Sunday—(take a break).

Remember here, the overall problem to be identified was how to get an offer of employment and what sub-problems that would consist of answering. When the time comes to get an interview, we can construct another one of these charts for *solving the problem* of whether to *accept* the new job offer (see decision-making in Chapter 8). Look above and examine how everything was broken down into manageable subtasks/problems.

This example demonstrated a steady plan of accountability and making substantial progress.

Exercise in Problem Solving

Instructions: Write down one of the problems you need to solve in the next zero to six months.

Start designing a program today to achieve those goals using the steps we discussed.

How will you make sure you are being held accountable? What is your timetable? Are you being realistic? Feel free to use the system we devised above if that will help you.

LARGER GOAL/PROBLEM TO BE SOLVED:

____

____

____

____

SMALLER/SUB GOAL/PROBLEM TO BE SOLVED:

____

____

____

____

ACCOUNTABILITY/RECALIBRATING:

____

____

____

____

YOUR OWN REWARD SYSTEM FOR FOLLOW-THROUGH

____

____

____

____

Creating Opportunities for "Successful Failures"

What do "successful failures" mean? In our lives, we encounter subjects, activities, and skills that we are not the world's #1 at, yet our "success" culture dominates over resiliency. We will NOT be good or the best at most things we attempt in life, so it is not about what we do *best* (although it is great if we are), but how we handle activities, situations in which we are

NOT the best. Most of us do not tolerate the distress related to not being the best very well. For example, if you are a cross-country runner and you have always been #1 in high school you can become accustomed to being "the best." However, what happens when you go to college and now you are ranked 30/33 runners? It's not that you suddenly became a horrible runner, but now you are surrounded by a higher level of runner. How would you handle this potentially perceived failure? How would you handle no longer being the best?

What happens when your identity is all about what you are the best at? It can be a dangerous, unstable situation, as there will ALWAYS be someone better than you. Let's talk about the example of "Michelle." Michelle is a 4.0 (unweighted), 1590 SAT, first-authored student in high school. She is an impressive student and candidate for a good university. She is accepted to a school such as Harvard. However, once she gets there, she is surrounded by students with equal, if not better credentials. What does this do to Michelle's identity and self-worth? Michelle no longer stands out as special or the best. She is now one of many people at the same level.

Resilience is our ability to adapt in the face of adversity or stress,[3,4] while distress tolerance is our ability to endure and withstand uncomfortable or negative emotions without making those feelings worse.[5,6] We want you to think of an activity or skill you know you are not strong in. For example, if you are not good at woodworking, you can use a YouTube video to make a birdhouse or build furniture from IKEA. Think of engaging in a project over the course of at least 45 minutes to a few hours each week that allows you to practice using your skills (e.g., breathing, progressive muscle relaxation, distress tolerance, and cognitive restructuring) to improve how you cope with feelings such as disappointment, sadness, and frustration related to performing poorly. In life, you will have plenty of experiences in which you do not perform well and will need to know how to cope with those, more than succeed. We want to strengthen your resilience and your distress tolerance.

Practice Failing Successfully!

A. Identify and practice an uncomfortable, distress-provoking activity or skill in which you know you will likely fail. Share your experience below. Try and not find humor in it. We want you to experience distress.

____

____

____

____

____

B. Write down what you learned.

   a. How did you cope with uncomfortable emotions?
   b. How can you pivot and use this experience to learn more about yourself or the situation in the future?

____

____

____

____

____

We are assuming that your executive functioning skills are within the limits of functionality with these tasks. However, if your attention, memory, and organizational skills are impaired, it will make these tasks very difficult. We would recommend a full evaluation of these skills by a neuropsychologist. They are the only type of doctors that can assess the function of the brain. Once you learn how your brain is functioning, you can then learn compensatory strategies to even the playing field with your peers.

References

1 Aaron T, Beck AT. *Cognitive therapy and the emotional disorders*. New York (NY): International Universities Press; 1976.
2 David D, Burns DD. Cognitive distortions and depression. In: Aaron T, Beck AT, editors. Cognitive therapy and the emotional disorders. New York (NY): International Universities Press; 1976. p. 235–278.
3 Ann S, Masten AS. Ordinary magic: resilience processes in development. *Am Psychol*. 2001;56(3):227–238.
4 Steven M, Southwick SM, George A, Bonanno GA, Ann S, Masten AS, Catherine Panter-Brick C, Yehuda R. Resilience definitions, theory, and challenges: interdisciplinary perspectives. *Eur J Psychotraumatol*. 2014;5:25338.
5 Leyro TM, Michael J, Zvolensky MJ, Bernstein A. Distress tolerance and psychopathological symptoms and disorders: a review of the empirical literature among adults. *Psychol Bull*. 2010;136(4):576–600.
6 Simons JS, Michael R, Gaher RM. The distress tolerance scale: development and validation of a self-report measure. *Motiv Emot*. 2005;29(2):83–102.

8 Decision-Making and Organizational Skills

After identifying problems and sub-problems, you then must begin making decisions. Making and following through on a decision is a very difficult task. We make decisions in daily life, both complicated and simple. We are going to break this process down for you and what that will look like once you are 22/23 years of age.

Decision-Making Skills

Decision-making is a foundational developmental task in young adulthood, with growing research suggesting that the ability to make effective, values-aligned decisions plays a critical role in promoting independence and preventing patterns described as *failure to launch*. Contrary to popular belief, decision-making is not a single skill, but rather a multi-dimensional capacity that includes cognitive, emotional, and social processes that evolve as we age.[1,2] It is rather complicated and very individualistic.

The decisions you've made so far in your young life have been helpful, but they will differ significantly from those required to become a successful and independent young adult. We often hear such phrases as, "I already know how to do this, this isn't useful for me, or why do I have to know things like this? It's so boring." When we, as clinicians, hear these statements, we automatically think these ARE the skills you need to learn. Ask any professional sports player. How often do you hear them claim they already know everything about their sport, dismissing further practice, or learning as "boring"? You don't! Why is this? Well, it's because even professionals, at all levels, and successful ones at that, recognize there is always something more to learn. We want to help you identify ways you can make and follow through with the best decision for your future self.

DOI: 10.4324/9781003649410-8

Steps to Take in Decision-Making

First, Identify the Decision You Would like to Make

The first step in effective decision-making is accurately identifying and defining the decision that needs to be made. Research on critical thinking highlights that individuals who clearly express the problem and gather information before acting tend to make more adaptive and flexible choices/decisions.[3] This is especially relevant to young adults who are often navigating high-stakes decisions related to relationships, education and career choices with more limited experience.

Use the same format we did in Chapter 7 with problem and sub-problem identification. Can you also think of a larger decision you must make? Can you identify the smaller decisions (e.g., what time to wake up in the morning) vs. a larger decision (e.g., what career to choose?). First, identify the decision to be made. We recommend identifying a smaller, more manageable decision to start. Keep with the same skill set as in Chapter 7, but instead of focusing on the problem, now narrow it to possible decisions in response to the problem.

Second, Weigh the Pros and Cons

Once each decision has been identified (again, under the umbrella of identifying the problem and sub-problems), carefully weigh the pros and cons to arrive at a well-informed choice.

The identified problem in this example is *arriving at class on time (8 am)*. One sub-problem is when to wake up. Now, you must *decide* what time to get up (e.g., 5, 6, 6:30 am, etc.) and identify the pros and cons of each of these decisions. Pros could be waking up with time to spare for other activities, such as exercise or making your own breakfast. A con could be not getting as much sleep if you were to set the alarm later. Evaluating/weighing your options is associated with higher life satisfaction and better emotional outcomes.[4] Maladaptive styles such as avoidance, impulsivity, or reliance on external pressures are linked to poorer outcomes.[4]

We also want to identify some of the major variables that contribute to our decisions: finances, location, and available support system. This is not an exhaustive list, but in our clinical experience we have found these variables to be the most relevant and frequently encountered/discussed.

Financial

When weighing pros and cons it is important you have a realistic view of your financial situation. Financial considerations have a direct impact on your stability and security. Positive financial outcomes may lead to increased savings, investment growth, and enhanced overall financial well-being. These involve an in-depth analysis of the monetary aspects associated with a decision. What does this mean? Well, this entails assessing the costs involved. For example, how much money will this realistically cost. Not how much you hope something will cost. A good rule of thumb is to overestimate by 1.5x. For example, if you expect a flight will cost $200, estimate $250 (which can include travel to and from the airport, as well as tax and fees of the flight). You can also examine potential returns or savings. Did you ever have a lemonade stand when you were a kid? You need to think about the cost of your time, efforts, and materials and then see how much you earned when the task was finished. Lastly, it is important to examine the impact on your overall financial stability. Frequently (i.e., at least 1x a week) check your spending and balances. Your electronic bank accounts will run one to two days behind the costs you incur in real life, so keep this in mind. This is why some people keep a check book with them; it can be more up to date than an online bank statement (check yours to view the tracking process).

Your financial health contributes to your ability to pursue personal and professional goals, affording a greater sense of control and flexibility. On the flip side, poor financial decisions may lead to debt, financial stress, or limitations in pursuing opportunities. Your financial health will determine your ability to follow through on your short and long-term goals.

Location

Second, significant decision-making goes into where you decide to live and work. Evaluating factors such as accessibility, amenities, and overall quality of life can guide the decision-making process. What do these mean? Well, what does it mean to live in a certain location? Do you want to live there or are your circumstances forcing you (e.g., work relocation)? Do you function better in a city vs. suburb vs. rural? You want to think of what you have been accustomed to, what you prefer (e.g., activities in a city, suburb, or country), how busy you like to be, and what you enjoy (e.g., city noises, vs. quiet of the country).

As the world has gotten smaller with the onset of social media, facetime, and artificial intelligence, our opportunities to live anywhere have been logistically easier. Take some time to think whether living in your country of origin is also for you (i.e., what do you like vs. dislike about your country of origin vs. other countries).

Support System/Relationships

Your social support network plays a significant role in your decision-making. Consider the availability of emotional, social, and practical support you receive from your family, friends, or other individuals. If you have positive outcomes with your social support network, you can improve your personal satisfaction, a deeper sense of connection, and the potential for personal growth through shared experiences. Conversely, decisions in this domain may also have consequences such as strained relationships, emotional distress, or changes in social dynamics. Considering the impact on your friendships, romantic partnerships, and overall social well-being is crucial to maintain a healthy and fulfilling personal life.

In high school and college, we focus heavily on our and others' social experiences. We take a genuine interest in our friends' lives. As we get older, jobs, children, and other adult responsibilities take over, and our social availability for others decreases. This is not necessarily out of a lack of caring, but more realism. Other things in life demand our attention and it is harder to provide support to our friends. So, what does this mean as a young adult (22/23 years old)? Your social support network will likely decrease in number, and your friends may not have as much time and space to support you individually. Again, this is likely not due to a lack of caring about you, but more the general demands of adulthood. Therefore, it is very important that you identify two to three people that can be alternated in terms of making you feel supported in life (with the intention of you providing them the same support as well).

You will also need to consider how your definition of romantic relationships will change (from high school and college) to around 22/23 years of age. There are innumerable books out there on the topic of romantic love. When you are 22/23 years or age, we recommend making decisions that put you on a growth trajectory. So, consider, are you in a relationship that limits your growth? Can you not move to a city you would like to because your romantic partner refuses to budge? Or maybe they would like to move with you but cannot because of a job. Social and romantic relationships can dictate a lot of our successes as a young, emerging adult and it is important to recognize when someone is helping you along a positive path vs. preventing or stifling your progress.

Outside of friends and romantic partners, decisions that positively influence the family domain can also result in strengthened bonds, improved communication, and a supportive social system. Sometimes your friends can become like family, and family members can also be your friends. Conversely, decisions that neglect family considerations may lead to strained relationships, conflicts, or feelings of isolation. Understanding any potential impact on your family dynamics, both immediate and extended, is crucial for maintaining a healthy and supportive social system.

By intentionally evaluating potential benefits and consequences in each of these life domains, you can make decisions that foster your own holistic well-being. This approach encourages a balanced and integrated perspective, ensuring that your choices align with your personal values, long-term aspirations, and the interconnected nature of logistical (financial and location) and social aspects of life.

Third, Deciding within a Timeline (e.g., Three to Six Months, One to Two Years, Five Years, etc.)

An effective decision-making process involves a comprehensive analysis of potential benefits and consequences (pros and cons) of various timelines, recognizing that the impact of a decision extends beyond the immediate future. By adopting a temporal perspective (i.e., incorporating factors as you perceive them in the past, present and future), you can make more informed and strategic choices that align with your long-term goals.

In the immediate timeline, you can assess the short-term outcomes and immediate repercussions of a decision. This involves considering the immediate benefits and potential challenges that may arise in the days or weeks following the decision. Moving forward to the three to six months' timeframe, the focus shifts to the mid-term consequences. This involves evaluating how the decision unfolds over a relatively short period, identifying any adjustments needed and ensuring that the chosen path remains on course. Expanding the horizon to one to two years allows you to ponder the longer-term consequences of a decision. This involves considering the sustainability of the decision, its impact on personal and professional growth, and any evolving circumstances that may need for you to adapt significantly.

At the five-year mark and beyond, you engage in foresight, thinking of the decision's enduring (long-lasting) effects. This includes considering potential opportunities that may arise, any necessary course corrections, and the overall alignment of the decision with evolving life goals. By examining potential benefits and consequences across these various timelines, you gain a "whole picture" understanding of the decision's ramifications. This approach helps to prevent short-sighted choices and encourages a more forward-thinking and strategic decision-making process that considers both immediate needs and long-term aspirations. It enables you to navigate the complexities of life with a sense of purpose and adaptability.

For example, at age 22/23 years of age, "Kay" gets accepted to medical school in the United Kingdom. It is an amazing opportunity, and they want to accept it immediately. However, they must decide, if I get licensed in the United Kingdom, in the long term, how does that limit their opportunities in coming back to the United States, where their family lives? Will they be able to practice or only conduct research? What will the licensing process look like? Is it realistic?

Just like "Kay," we can get caught up in the energy and pace of making decisions without thinking through the long-term effects or consequences. We cannot predict every obstacle or outcome, and that will require our distress tolerance skills (learned earlier in Chapter 5), but we do need to think them through.

Taking an Honest Look at Avoiding a Decision (Pros/Cons)

Although we are proponents against avoiding, sometimes avoiding/delaying a decision can have an upside. Let us honestly explore the pros and cons of delaying or altogether avoiding decision-making:

Pros of Avoiding or Delaying a Decision

1 Additional time for information gathering: Delaying a decision can provide an opportunity to gather more information, leading to a more informed choice. This is particularly beneficial in complex situations where more data or insights are needed.
2 Need for emotional distance and effective coping: Taking a step back and delaying a decision may allow emotions to settle down, which can enable you to make a more rational and objective choice. This is crucial in situations where emotions might cloud your judgment.
3 Opportunity for reflection: Avoiding an immediate decision provides for more time for introspection and reflection. This can lead to deeper insight and understanding of your own personal values and priorities, which contributes to better decision-making. Be careful in allowing yourself too much time. Give yourself a specific amount (one to two days, one week), so you do not fall into the never-ending avoidance category.
4 Not making a rushed decision: By deliberately avoiding (again, for a prescribed period), we can also prevent ourselves from making hasty and impulsive decisions that have negative consequences. Take the time to carefully weigh your options and make thoughtful decisions.

Cons of Avoiding or Delaying a Decision

1 Missed opportunities: Procrastinating on decisions can result in missed opportunities. Sometimes we think or say to ourselves, "I will just return to this," but self-accountability is very hard to achieve, as we have already established. Certain chances and opportunities do have time constraints (e.g., due dates) and delaying a decision might mean giving up these chances for growth or achievement.
2 Increased emotionality (stress and anxiety): Prolonged indecision can lead us to experience a great deal of stress and anxiety. The uncertainty associated with delaying decisions may contribute to a sense of unease and hinder your overall well-being.[5]
3 Impact on relationships: Avoiding decisions in the realm of interpersonal relationships can strain your connections. It may lead to frustration or

disappointment on the part of one or both parties. How would you feel if an employer said they needed Six months to let you know whether you have a job? That would cause some significant problems in your life.
4 Procrastination habits: Repeatedly avoiding decisions can cultivate a habit of procrastination. Over time, this habit may hinder your personal and professional growth and lead to a pattern of indecisiveness and overall avoidance.
5 Compounding Issues: Avoiding small decisions can sometimes lead to the compounding of issues, turning what could have been a relatively simple decision into a more complex one over time.

In summary, the choice to avoid or delay a decision should be strategic and context dependent. While it can provide benefits such as additional time for reflection and information gathering, it is essential to be mindful of the potential downsides, such as missed opportunities, increased stress, and strained relationships. Striking a balance between careful consideration and timely action is key to effective decision-making.

Acting on Your Decision

The next and most important step is *acting* on your decision. Translating your intentions into meaningful actions requires careful planning, resource management, and adaptability. Effective implementation of your decisions requires a balance between flexibility and stability so you can adjust to unpredictable changes along the way. Decisions remain intentions if they are not acted upon. While following through with the decision, make sure to use your distress tolerance skills. We all must accept that no decision will ever be 100% right.

Examining the Consequences of Your Decisions and How to Re-calibrate and Move Forward

Once the decision has been fully implemented, take the time to evaluate the overall process and result. What worked and what did not? Evaluating the outcomes of your decision, both positive and negative, and recalibrating from there is an important part of this process. Emotional processing plays a key role in this phase, as you will integrate this into your own personal experience and accordingly adjust your future decisions.[4] Re-examination and recalibrating help you build resilience and underscores the importance of maintaining a dynamic, rather than rigid, approach to life planning.[1,6] Receiving constructive feedback from others can highlight areas you need to improve or slightly alter, which can impact the implementation process moving forward.

Devising a Flexible *Plan*: What Is Your Timeline?

An important extension of effective decision-making is the ability to translate an individual decision into a flexible, actionable plan. Instead of viewing decisions as isolated events, research suggests that adaptive functioning in young adulthood is supported by the capacity to think in structured yet adjustable timelines, integrating both short-term action and long-term direction.[1,6]

Short-Term Planning: Six Months–One Year

This is the foundational stage where momentum and a sense of agency (owning your own part) are built. As such, it is important for goals to be manageable to increase the chances of success and build self-confidence in your decision-making skills. At this stage, your decisions will lead to direct observational changes in your life. From a research perspective, short-term planning supports behavioral activation (i.e., moving your body into goal-oriented action) and follow-through, which are key to preventing avoidance patterns.[4]

Here are a few questions to ask yourself at this stage:

What next specific steps are needed to accomplish my goals?

____

____

What routines will support my decision?

____

____

What resources do I need?

____

____

"Mid-Term" Planning: One to Two Years

"Mid-term" is when outcomes emerge, patterns start to be available for your own observation, and you receive data on your internal experience. For example, you may start to notice advancements in your career or increasing financial stability and your sense of life satisfaction increasing. This is also the stage where re-calibration may be necessary if you notice that you are not progressing the way you desire. Here are a few questions to ask yourself about your decisions at this stage:

Is the path I am on sustainable?

What changes are needed in my approach based on what I have learned so far?

Long-Term: Three to Five Years and on

Long-term decisions involve developing a broader vision of one's life goals, while maintaining flexibility in how that vision is achieved. Research suggests that adaptive decision-making is not about predicting the future with certainty, but about maintaining a directional compass that can guide your ever-evolving choices.[4] Here are a few questions to ask yourself at this stage:

What kind of life am I working toward?

What is important to me across different areas of my life (relationships, career, etc.)?

Decision-Making Worksheet

In this section, you are going to put everything we have discussed into practice. Let us start with an example of a decision you might be faced with at 22/23 years of age.

You have applied for 15 jobs. You received four offers of employment. How would you go about making the decision of what job to accept?

Step 1: Identify the Decision

What decision are you trying to make?

What feels clear or unclear about this decision?

____

____

Step 2: Clarify Your Options

List the main options you are considering:

Option 1: ______________________________________
Option 2: ______________________________________
Option 3 (if applicable): ______________________________

Step 3: Weigh the Pros & Cons (in Four Areas)

Financial Impact

What are the financial pros and cons of each option? (Figure 8.1)

	Option	Pros	Cons
1			
2			
3			

Figure 8.1 A blank three-row table for decision-making with columns labeled "Option," "Pros," and "Cons." Rows are numbered 1, 2, and 3, providing space to compare three different choices.

Location

How does each option affect where you live and your environment? Pros/ cons?

	Option	Pros	Cons
1			
2			
3			

Figure 8.1 A blank three-row table for decision-making with columns labeled "Option," "Pros," and "Cons." Rows are numbered 1, 2, and 3, providing space to compare three different choices.

Support System

How does each option impact your access to support (family, friends, community)? Pros/Cons?

	Option	Pros	Cons
1			
2			
3			

Figure 8.1 A blank three-row table for decision-making with columns labeled "Option," "Pros," and "Cons." Rows are numbered 1, 2, and 3, providing space to compare three different choices.

Step 4: Outcomes of the Decisions over Time

Immediate (Zero to Three months):

____

____

Three to Six months:

____

____

One to Two years:

____

____

Five + years:

____

____

Step 5: What Happens If You Delay a Decision?

What are the potential benefits of waiting?

____

____

What are the potential costs or risks of waiting?

____

____

What might happen if nothing changes in six months?

____

____

Step 6: Make Your Decision

Based on everything above, what decision/s are you ready to take action on?

____

____

What values or priorities is this decision based on?

____

____

Step 7: Taking Action

What are the first three concrete steps you will take?

1 ____
2 ____
3 ____

When will you start?

____
____

Step 8: Plan for Reflection and Adjustment

How will you evaluate if this decision is working?

____
____

When will you check in with yourself? (e.g., One month, Three months)

____
____

If things do not go as expected, how will you adjust?

____
____

Final Reflection

What did you learn about yourself through this process?

____
____

What helped you move forward?

____
____

Organizational Skills

Organization skills are one of the core components of independent living. These skills include planning, prioritization, time management, and task completion. Organization skills fall under the big umbrella of executive functioning processes such as working memory, cognitive flexibility, and self-control, which continue to develop into early adulthood.[7,8] When these skills are underdeveloped, for various reasons, individuals may be overwhelmed by life tasks (e.g., difficulty initiating tasks) and can develop patterns of avoidance leading to that feeling of being "stuck." In this context, disorganization is not just poor planning but rather a broader difficulty turning intentions into action. Developing effective organizational skills becomes essential for reducing your cognitive load (i.e., how much you are managing and balancing in your mind), increasing a sense of independence, and increasing consistency in your goal fulfillment.

Themes of Organization (Systems by Which We Can Organize Tasks)

Organization by Time (Timelines and Deadlines)

One of the most accessible ways to organize tasks is by anchoring them to time either through deadlines or recurring schedules. Tasks such as paying bills, completing work or school assignments, and managing weekly responsibilities naturally lend themselves to time-based organization. Research suggests that structuring tasks around time increases perceived control and reduces stress, as it provides clear expectations for when tasks should be completed.[9] Additionally, time management is less about "doing more" and more about making intentional decisions about how to use available time.[9] Establishing predictable rhythms such as a weekly planning session or a designated day for administrative tasks can reduce fatigue in making your decisions and increase your consistency. Over time, these patterns can become habitual, making organization feel less effortful and more automatic, just like forming a prosocial habit (e.g., brushing your teeth).

Organization by Importance/Prioritization

Effective organization also requires the ability to prioritize tasks based on their importance rather than solely on urgency. While urgent tasks often demand immediate attention, they are not always aligned with your long-term values. It is easy to get distracted by what is right in front of you. Research indicates that people are more likely to follow through on tasks they perceive as meaningful or valuable.[10] Researchers have also found it is important for us to direct our attention toward high-value tasks, even when they are less immediately rewarding.[11] In practice, this means learning to identify which areas, such as financial stability, relationships, family responsibilities, or personal growth, deserve focused attention and the order in which we need to address them. Without intentional prioritization, it is easy to avoid difficult but important tasks. This can lead us to procrastinate more, leading to higher levels of stress, and perpetuating the cycle of avoidance.

Organization by Grouping/Task Batching

Another effective organizational strategy involves grouping similar tasks together, often referred to as *task batching*. Rather than switching between unrelated tasks, which increases cognitive load (the amount of information in your mind you must juggle at once), batching allows individuals to focus on one type of activity at a time. Research shows that frequent task-switching reduces efficiency and increases mental fatigue, whereas grouping similar tasks can improve productivity and sustain attention.[12,13] For example, setting aside time to handle all financial tasks at once (e.g., paying bills, reviewing budgets, etc.), completing multiple household chores in one block, or dedicating time to health-related activities can create a sense of momentum. This approach not only improves efficiency but also reduces the mental clutter that comes from constantly shifting focus. Do not stray from completing half of one category and then back to the other. Stay with the task at hand until it is completed.

Time Allocation and Avoiding Overextension

While organizing tasks is important, it is equally critical to realistically allocate time and avoid overcommitting. Many individuals struggle not because they lack awareness of what needs to be done, but because they attempt to do too much at once. Research suggests that intentional time allocation is associated with greater well-being and a stronger sense of control, while overextension (taking on too much at the same time) is linked to increased stress and burnout.[14,15] Effective organization involves recognizing your limits and planning accordingly, rather than creating overly ambitious schedules that are difficult to sustain. This may involve setting aside small, manageable blocks of time (think 10–15 minutes) to begin organizing tasks. Building in flexibility and allowing for rest are also essential, as sustainable systems require balance rather than constant productivity.

A critical component of building organizational skills is developing awareness of your current systems. You must continually self-monitor and reflect. These processes are key in self-regulation, allowing you to evaluate what is working and identify areas for improvement.[16,17] Rather than approaching organizing systems with judgment, we encourage you to take a curious and observational stance: What systems do you already have in place? Where do things tend to break down? What feels overwhelming or unclear? This process helps shift organization from a reactive effort to a more intentional and adaptive practice. Even small insights can lead to meaningful changes when you apply them in the same way over time.

Organizational Skills Worksheet

Step 1: Observe Your Current System

Look at your current environment and routines (room, schedule, responsibilities). What system/s do you currently have in place?

____

____

What is organized or disorganized?

____

____

What *feels* disorganized or overwhelming?

____

____

Step 2: Organize by Time (Deadlines/Due Dates and Routines)

List your regular responsibilities:

Daily Tasks:

____

____

Weekly Tasks:

____

____

Monthly Tasks (e.g., bills):

____

____

Do you currently have a system for tracking these?
☐ Yes ☐ No

If yes, what works?

____

____

If not, what could you try?

____

____

Step 3: Prioritize by Importance

What are the most important areas of your life right now? (Rank top Three)

1 ____
2 ____
3 ____

Which tasks are important to you but you avoid them?

____

____

Why do you think you avoid them?

____

____

Step 4: Grouping Similar Tasks (Batching)

Group your tasks into categories:

☐ Chores / Home

☐ Health / Exercise

☐ Finances

☐ Work / School

☐ Relationships / Family

☐ Other: ____________________

Pick one category to focus on this week:

____

____

When will you work on this group of tasks?

____

____

Step 5: Plan Your Time (Avoid Overloading Your Schedule)

How much time can you realistically dedicate to organizing this week?

____

____

What is one small, manageable goal?

____

____

What might get in the way?

____

____

How can you keep this realistic?

____

____

Step 6: Improving Your Environment

Look at your physical space (e.g., bedroom). What area needs the most attention?

____

____

What is one small change you can make?

____

____

How will this make things easier for you?

____

____

Step 7: Take Action

List Three small steps you will take this week:

1 ____
2 ____
3 ____

When will you start?

Step 8: Reflect and Adjust

At the end of the week:

What worked?

What did not work? Why?

What will you adjust next week?

Step 9: Build a Simple Routine

Choose one routine to repeat:

☐ Daily (Five to Ten minutes)

☐ Weekly reset

☐ Monthly check-in

What will your routine be?

When will you do it?

Final Reflection

What did you learn about how you function best (i.e., what is your organizational system)?

What is one thing you will keep doing or change?

___

___

References

1 Choudhury NA, Saravanan P. An integrative review on unveiling the causes and effects of decision fatigue to develop a multi-domain conceptual framework. Front Cognit. 2025;4.

2 Moutoussis M, Dolan RJ, Dayan P. How people use social information to find out what to want in the paradigmatic case of intertemporal preferences. *Nat Commu*. 2016;12:5677.

3 Shih PC, Pérez-Santiago Á, Peña D, Wazne D, Román S. Jumping to conclusions: mechanisms of cognitive control in decision-making under uncertainty. *Behav Sci*. 2025;15(2):226.

4 Cardona-Isaza ADJ, Montoya-Castilla I, Trujillo A. Decis ion-making styles, prosociality, and behavioral difficulties in adolescent offenders: the mediating role of life satisfaction and emotional experiences. *Behav Sci*. 2025;15(1):80.

5 Shih PC, Pérez-Santiago Á, Peña D, Wazne D, Román S. Jumping to conclusions: mechanisms of cognitive control in decision-making under uncertainty. *Behav Sci*. 2025;15(2):226. 1–19.

6 Billore S, Anisimova T, Vrontis D. Self-regulation and goal-directed behavior: a systematic literature review, public policy recommendations, and research agenda. *J Bus Res*. 2023;156.

7 Best JR, Miller PH. A developmental perspective on executive function. *Child Dev*. 2010;92(6):2249–2263.

8 Diamond A. Executive functions. *Annu Rev Psychol*. 2013;64(1):135–168.

9 Aeon B, Aguinis H. It's about time: new perspectives and insights on time management. *Acad Manage Perspect*. 2017;35(2):197–213.

10 Milyavskaya M, Inzlicht M. Attentional and motivational mechanisms of self-control. In: de Ridder DTD, Adriaanse MA, Fujita K, editors. *The Routledge International Handbook of self-control in health and well-being*. Abingdon: Routledge; 2018. p. 11–23.

11 Baumeister RF, Tice DM. Ego depletion is the best replicated finding in all of social psychology. *Sch J Psychol Behav Sci*. 2022;6(2).

12 Mark G, Gudith D, Klocke U. The cost of interrupted work: more speed and stress. In *Proceedings of the SIGCHI conference on Human Factors in Computing Systems*, Florence, Italy; 2008. p. 107–110.

13 Puranik H, Koopman J, Vough HC. Pardon the interruption: an integrative review and future research agenda for research on work interruptions. *J Manage*. 2020;46(6):806–842.

14 Häfner A, Stock A, Oberst V. Decreasing students' stress through time management training: an intervention study. *Eur J Psychol Edu*. 2015;36:353–371.

15 Sonnentag S. The recovery paradox: portraying the complex interplay between job stressors, lack of recovery, and poor well-being. *Res Organ Behav.* 2018;38:169–185.
16 Panadero E. A review of self-regulated learning: six models and four directions for research. *Front Psychol.* 2017;12:422.
17 Zimmerman BJ. Self-regulated learning: theories, measures, and outcomes. In: Wright JD, editor. *International encyclopedia of the social and behavioral science.* Oxford: Elsevier; 2015. p. 541–546.

9 Using Skills Instead of Passion to Determine Life Satisfaction

In this chapter, you are going to focus on your skills and how to leverage them for success. We will also help you clearly differentiate between *skills* and *passion*. We want you to make decisions based on a realistic understanding of your abilities and not just what you feel excited about at the moment. While it feels amazing to love what you do, it is unrealistic to expect that you will enjoy every part and every day of your work all the time. In fact, most people do not. What tends to matter over time is whether you are effective, capable, and making progress—what we would define as *mastering*. By identifying and pursuing opportunities that align with your strengths, you position yourself to accomplish goals more efficiently while also creating personal satisfaction, financial stability, and a sense of emotional and logistical security, all of which are strongly linked to your long-term well-being.

How to Define "Skills"

Skills are abilities you have developed through consistent effort, repetition, and practice. They are things/activities you can do well and competently even when you do not feel particularly motivated. You have a level of mastery over them, and even if you do not enjoy them, they can still be valuable to you. When we talk about *skills* in this context, we are referring to the abilities you would typically list on your resume or CV, things you can demonstrate, apply, and rely on in real-world situations. These might include physical skills, technical/programmatic skills, communication skills, problem-solving skills, organizational skills, computational skills, or anything else that helps you do well in your daily life or work.

Many people are surprised to learn that you are more likely to feel satisfied doing something you are good at than something you simply "love" of which you struggle. When you perform well at something, you naturally experience a sense of accomplishment. Over time, that sense of

DOI: 10.4324/9781003649410-9

accomplishment builds confidence and encourages your willingness to keep going especially when things get difficult. This is different from *passion*. *Passion* often feels exciting in the moment, but it can be inconsistent. Mastered skills, however, are stable. They also grow stronger with practice and create a reliable sense of progress.

Feeling competent is a human need, and when that need is met, we experience greater motivation, satisfaction, and persistence.[1] In other words, we are wired to *feel* good when we *are* good at something. This is why people often report growing to like or even love things they initially felt neutral about, simply because they became skilled at them over time. In contrast, relying solely on *passion* without building *skill* can lead to frustration, inconsistency, and even burnout.

This does not mean *passion* is unimportant, it simply means it should not be the *only* or *main* factor guiding your decisions. A more sustainable approach is to ask:

- What am I capable of doing well?
- Where can I realistically improve with practice?
- What opportunities allow me to use my strengths while continuing to grow?

When you start with your skills, you create a foundation of competence. From there, satisfaction and sometimes even passion can develop naturally and simultaneously. However, satisfaction has a longer shelf life, while passion frequently waxes and wanes over time. In other words, passion is not very dependable.

Use the examples below to get ideas about the kinds of skills you may already have in different areas of your life. You will explore your own skills more directly in the exercise that follows.

Academic Skills

☐ I can keep up with assignments; I can study for tests
☐ I can write essays or complete projects
☐ I can meet organize my assignments and meet deadlines
☐ I can figure things out when I don't understand

Responsibility and Time Skills

☐ I show up where I need to be on time
☐ I can balance multiple things (school, friends, activities)
☐ I follow a schedule (even loosely)
☐ I get things done even when I do not feel like it

Work and Real-Life Skills

☐ I can use email/Google Docs
☐ I can learn new apps or systems quickly
☐ I consistently follow instructions from teachers, coaches, or bosses
☐ I've worked or helped in a job-like setting

Communication Skills

☐ I can talk to people my age
☐ I can talk to adults
☐ I can ask questions
☐ I can explain my thoughts
☐ I can work in a group

Problem-Solving Skills

☐ I can figure things out on my own
☐ I can handle unexpected situations
☐ I adjust when plans change
☐ I learn from mistakes

Social Skills

☐ I can make new or keep friends
☐ People can rely on me
☐ I support others
☐ I can handle conflict

Home-Based Life Skills

☐ I can clean or organize
☐ I can do laundry or basic chores
☐ I help at home (e.g., make meals)
☐ I can manage basic daily routines

Financial/Money Skills

☐ I can save money
☐ I think before spending
☐ I understand basic money choices and know how to balance my accounts (if you have them)

Other Interests/Skills

☐ Gaming (strategy, teamwork)
☐ Social media/content creation
☐ Sports
☐ Music/art/design
☐ Planning events or organizing things

As you look over the example of skills, you may notice that some of them feel interesting, while others do not, and that is completely expected. This is where *passion* often enters the conversation, and where it is important to understand what it can and cannot do for you.

What Is "Passion?"

Passion is something, whether it is a job, activity, or topic, that you feel a strong sense of interest, excitement, or positive emotions toward. It can feel energizing and motivating, especially at the beginning. One important thing to understand about *passion* is that it is inconsistent, meaning it naturally waxes and wanes over time. Your level of passion can shift depending on your mood, stress level, environment, energy, and even how familiar something has become. What once felt exciting can start to feel routine, and that does not mean something is wrong, it is just how humans operate.

Because passion is so emotion-driven, it can be unreliable as a sole guide for action. During times when passion is high, it is easier to stay engaged and motivated. When passion dips, as it inevitably will, it can suddenly feel much harder to show up, stay consistent, or follow through on plans. This is where many people get stuck. If you expect yourself to always feel excited or inspired, then a normal drop in motivation can start to feel like a sign that you are on the "wrong path."

Passion can create unrealistic internal expectations about how you "should" feel. For example, a common belief that comes up is: "I need to love my job all the time, or else it's not right for me." The problem with this belief is that it does not match how motivation works. Passion requires a great deal of maintenance, most being unrealistic, which can lead you to feel frustration, self-doubt, and even burnout.

A more realistic way to think about passion is that it is a helpful bonus, not a requirement. It can make things feel easier and more enjoyable, but it is not what sustains long term or your long-term effort. Consistency is much more often driven by structure, habits, and a sense of competence.

In fact, many people build passion after they have spent time developing confidence/mastery in their skills.

So instead of asking, "Do I love this all the time?" a more helpful question is:

- Can I still show up even when I do not feel like it?
- Is this meaningful or worthwhile, even on the days it feels hard?

Shifting your expectations in this way allows you to stay engaged through the natural ups and downs of motivation, rather than interpreting those dips as failure or a sign to quit (either a job, career, or a task at hand).

Before moving forward, it is important to take a step back and get a clear focus or idea on what you already bring to the table. Many people overlook their own skills because they seem "basic" or because they do not feel exciting. However, these everyday abilities are often the strongest foundation for growth, as feeling capable and effective is closely tied to motivation and overall well-being.[2] The worksheet below is designed to help you identify your skills in a simple, practical way without getting caught up in whether you feel passionate about them. The goal is to focus on what you can do consistently, so you have something steady to build on.

Skills over Passion Worksheet

Step 1: Shift Your Mindset

Before we begin, reflect, and answer the following questions:

What have you been taught about passion and work (whether academic or job-related)?

____

____

Have you ever felt like you needed to "love" something to keep doing it?

____

____

How has that belief helped or hurt you?

____

____

Step 2: Identify Your Skills (see examples on previous worksheet)

List skills you already have (things you can do competently—even if you do not *love* them):

____

____

Think about:

- School/work tasks
- Things others rely on you for
- Things you've improved at over time

Step 3: Evidence of Your Skills

Pick two to three skills and answer:

A. Skill:

____

How do you know you are good at this?

____

B. Skill:

____

How do you know you are good at this?

____

C. Skill:

____

How do you know you are good at this?

____

Step 4: Separate Skills from Passion

Look at your skills list. For each skill, ask:

Do I enjoy this? ☐ Yes ☐ No ☐ Sometimes

Am I still able to do it well? ☐ Yes ☐ No ☐ Sometimes

What do you notice?

____

Step 5: Identify Opportunities Based on Skills

Where could you use your skills right now? (job, school, home, etc.)

____

Which skill feels most reliable for you to use consistently?

____

Step 6: Build Consistency

What is one small action you can take this week using your skills?

____

When will you do it?

____

Step 7: Reflect on Competence

After taking action, answer:

How did it feel to complete something you are good at?

____

Did you notice any sense of accomplishment?

____

Final Reflection

What is one thing you are learning about skills vs. passion?

What will you focus on moving forward?

Many of us have picked up incorrect beliefs about *passion* (e.g., "Oh, I am so passionate about"—fill in the blank), which sounds helpful on the surface but can actually hold us back. Before we take a closer look at these ideas, take a moment to reflect on what you have been taught or assumed about passion.

Reflection

Use the exercise below to explore how your beliefs about passion may be influencing your avoidance, inconsistency, or decision-making. Try to complete it without overthinking or trying to be "right."

Step 1: Check Your Thinking

Which of these statements do you believe? (Check all that apply)

☐ I should love what I do *all* the time

☐ If I'm not motivated, it's not for me

☐ If I get bored, I should quit

☐ I need to find my passion first

☐ If it is right, it should feel easy

Step 2: Reality Check

Pick one belief and answer:

Belief I have had:

How has this belief affected your actions?

Did it help you move forward/give you momentum or hold you back?

____

Let us pause here and compare some of these common beliefs about passion with what tends to be true in real life.

What people say (Myth)	*What's actually true (Fact)*
I should love what I do all the time	No one does—everyone has days where they're not feeling it
If I'm not motivated, it means it's not for me	Motivation comes and goes—you can still show up without it
Passion will make me successful	Being consistent and getting good at something matters more
If I get bored, I should quit	Getting bored is normal and doesn't mean you are on the wrong path
I need to find my passion before I start anything	You usually find what you like after you try things and get better at them
If it's right for me, it should feel easy	Most things that matter take effort, even if you enjoy them
I shouldn't do things I don't like	Some of the best opportunities come from things you don't love at first
If I don't feel excited, I'm doing something wrong	You're not—feelings change, but progress still counts

Step 3: Challenge the Passion Myth

Rewrite your belief in a more realistic way:
Old belief: ______________________________________
New belief: ______________________________________

Step 4: Action Challenge

What is one thing you can do this week—even if you don't feel like it?

____

When will you do it?

How will you hold yourself accountable?

References

1 Deci EL, Olafsen AH, Ryan RM. Self-determination theory in work organizations: the state of a science. *Annu Rev Organ Psychol Organ Behav.* 2017;4:19–43.
2 Ryan RM, Deci EL. Self-determination theory and the facilitation of intrinsic motivation, social development, and well-being. *Am Psychol.* 2000;55(1):68.

10 Goal Setting

Making Specific but Flexible Plans

Defining a Goal

In Chapter 9, we focused on using your skills, not just your feelings, to make decisions. Now that you have a clearer sense of what you are capable of, the next step is figuring out how to use those skills to build something meaningful. That starts with setting goals. Goals are broader than what we have addressed throughout this book thus far.

Defining a *Goal*?

A *goal* is something you want to work toward or accomplish. It gives you a sense of direction, like a guide for where you're going and what you're trying to build in your life. Goals do not have to be huge or life-changing (at least not right away). They can be small, everyday things or bigger long-term plans. For example, a goal could be:

- finishing your assignments on time this week
- getting better at talking to people
- improving your grades in one class
- saving some money
- or even just building a better routine

Goals can show up in all areas of your life like school, friendships, family, health, hobbies, or just becoming a better version of yourself. You might want to learn something new, get better at something you already do, or make a change that helps your life feel more manageable.

The important thing about goals is that they give you something to move toward. When you have a goal, even a small one, it is easier to stay focused and make decisions (what we addressed in Chapter 8). Every time you follow through and achieve a goal, no matter how small, you start to

DOI: 10.4324/9781003649410-10

build confidence, discipline, and a sense of accomplishment. Over time, those small steps add up and that is how real progress happens. The virtue of patience is a necessity in accomplishing your goals, as it does not happen all at once, but little by little. Progress comes through setbacks, small steps forward, and sustained determination and grit. We mentioned grit and perseverance earlier in Chapter 3. Think of perseverance as not giving up in the short-term and grit as not giving up in the long-term. For example, someone who studies hard for one test has perseverance and one who worked for 15 years toward their Ph.D. has grit. Grit and perseverance have both been found to be linked to academic, athletic, and career advancement in the short and long-term.[1,2]

Goal Setting

So now that you know what a *goal* is, let us talk about how to set one in a way that you can follow through with success. Setting goals is an essential part of personal growth and achievement. Research consistently shows that clearly defined goals provide direction, motivation, and a clear path to success whereas vague or overly ambitious goals tend to lead to frustration and inconsistency.[3] In other words, goals work best when they are clear, realistic, and actionable. A key part of effective goal setting is making sure your goals are realistic based on where you are right now. People are more likely to follow through on goals they believe are achievable and aligned with their current abilities, time, and energy.[4] For example, do *NOT* say "I'd like to run a marathon tomorrow" when all you can do is one mile today. A more effective approach would be to gradually increase your distance over time. This is where pacing becomes important. Instead of aiming too high too quickly, focus on steady, manageable progress. Look at your current schedule and ask yourself: *What can I realistically commit to this week?* Apply your decision-making skills by setting goals that you're reasonably confident—around 80%—you can successfully follow through on. Keep goals challenging enough to promote your growth, while still being relatively achievable. It can be hard to tell the difference between a goal that works and one that does not—so let's look at some real-life examples.

Unrealistic goal	Realistic goal
I'm going to get straight *A*'s this semester	I'm going to improve my grade in math from a *C* to a *B* by studying three more times a week
I'll start working out every day for an hour	I will work out for 20 minutes, 3 times a week
I am going to stop procrastinating	I will start my assignments at least 30 minutes earlier for at least 3 out of 7 days this week

Unrealistic goal	Realistic goal
I will save $1,000 in one month	I will save $20–50 per week
I am going to be more confident	I will speak up at least once in class this week
I will fix my sleep habits starting tonight	I will go to bed 30 minutes earlier 3 nights this week
I will start eating healthy	I will add one serving of fruits or vegetables each day
I will make a lot of new friends	I will start one conversation with someone new this week
I will finish all my missing assignments today	I will complete 1–2 missing assignments today
I am going to run a marathon soon	I will run 1–2 miles, 2 times this week

Another critical part of the process involves breaking larger goals into *smaller, specific goals.* Smaller goals make progress feel more manageable and allow you to build momentum through consistent wins.[3] For example, instead of setting a goal like "get in shape," you might start with "walk for 15 minutes three times this week." These smaller steps act as building blocks toward your larger goal.

If you are not meeting your smaller goals that does not mean you have failed. It means it is time to *recalibrate*. In fact, adjusting goals and strategies based on feedback is a key part of long-term success.[5] Remember that you can reference Chapter 7 (problem solving) and Chapter 8 (decision-making and organizational skills) to help you reassess your goals. Some helpful questions to ask yourself at this point might be:

- Do I need to slow down?
- Do I need to make this goal more specific?
- Am I being realistic?
- Do I need additional support or accountability?

Another important piece of goal setting is how you respond to challenges along the way. Negative thoughts such as *"I'm not doing enough"* or *"I already messed up"* can quickly derail progress if left unchecked. Instead of giving up, practice shifting your mindset. Starting again is more helpful than stopping completely. Challenging negative self-talk and replacing it with more balanced, supportive thoughts can help you stay consistent even when your motivation is low. This is such an important skill to have (and you can review it in Chapter 7) because motivation and persistence are influenced not just by the goal itself, but by how you interpret setbacks and manage your emotions over time.

Finally, do not underestimate the power of *rewards*. Recognizing your progress, especially what may feel like small wins, helps build confidence and keeps you motivated over time. This can be as simple as acknowledging your effort, tracking your progress, or giving yourself a small reward when you meet a goal. Both internal rewards (feeling accomplished) and external rewards (treating yourself) can strengthen your follow-through and sustain long-term behavior change. By setting goals in a structured yet adaptable way—defining clear objectives, pacing yourself, breaking them into manageable steps, making adjustments when necessary, and reinforcing progress—you build a system that fosters not only achievement, but sustained growth and consistency.

Before setting your goals, there is one more important thing to understand—*where you are starting from.* Not everyone is at the same place when it comes to making changes. Some people are just thinking about change, while others are already taking action. This is where assessing what "stage of change" you are at can be helpful.[6] Progress happens in steps, not all at once. Let us look at these steps with examples.

____

____

____

____

Stage 1: Not Ready

"I'm not really thinking about changing this right now."
Example: "I know I stay up late, but I don't care yet."

Stage 2: Thinking About It

"I know I should probably change this... but I haven't started."
Example: "I should probably fix my sleep schedule."

Stage 3: Getting Ready

"I'm starting to make a plan."
Example: "Maybe I'll try going to bed earlier this week."

Stage 4: Taking Action

"I'm actually doing it."
Example: "I went to bed earlier 3 nights this week."

Stage 5: Keeping It Going

"I'm trying to stick with it."
Example: "I've been keeping a better sleep routine for 3 weeks now."

Take a moment to think about one area of your life you might want to change or improve. This is not about setting a goal yet—it is just about accepting and understanding where you are right now.

Reflection Exercise

Pick one area you want to improve:

___

___

Which stage are you in?

☐ Not ready
☐ Thinking about it
☐ Getting ready
☐ Taking action
☐ Keeping it going

What would a realistic next step look like for this stage?

___

___

Now that you have a better understanding of how to set realistic and effective goals as well as where you are starting from, the next step is to put it all into practice. The following worksheet with examples is designed to help you break down the process of setting goals.

Goal-Setting Worksheet

Instructions: Use this worksheet to set realistic goals, pace yourself, and stay motivated. Follow each section carefully and take time to reflect on your progress.

Step 1: Define Your Goal

What is your main goal? (Be specific.) Example: "I want to run a 5k race in three months."

___

___

___

___

___

Why is this goal important to you? (What will it bring to your life?)

___

___

___

___

___

Step 2: Make Your Goal Realistic

Is your goal achievable based on where you are now? (Be honest.) Example: "I can currently run 1 mile comfortably, so a 5K in three months is reasonable."

___

___

___

___

___

If your goal seems too ambitious, how can you adjust to make it more realistic?

___

___

___

___

___

Step 3: Pace Yourself Slowly

Look at your schedule. How much time can you realistically dedicate to working toward this goal? *Example: "I can train for 30 minutes, three times a week."*

___

___

___

___

___

What is your confidence level (One to Ten) that you can stick to this plan? If it's below eight, adjust your plan to increase your chances of success.

___

___

___

___

___

Step 4: Set Up Smaller, Achievable Goals

List at least three smaller goals that will help you reach your big goal:

Example: Run 1.5 miles non-stop by next week.
Increase my running distance by 0.5 miles every two weeks.
Complete a 2.5-mile run by the end of the second month.

____
____
____
____

Step 5: Recalibrate If Needed

If you struggle to meet a small goal, how will you adjust?
Example: "If I can't increase my running distance by 0.5 miles, I'll increase it by 0.25 miles instead."

____
____
____
____

What might be holding you back? (Check all that apply.)

- Going too fast
- Not setting specific enough goals
- Lack of accountability/support
- Negative self-talk or discouragement
- Other: ______________________________

Step 6: Challenge Negative Thoughts

What negative thoughts might come up if you struggle with your goal?
Example: "I'll never be able to do this."

____
____
____
____
____

How can you reframe those thoughts to be helpful to you (e.g., "I am making progress, even if it's slower than I expected")?

____
____
____
____

What are three positive affirmations you can tell yourself?
Example: "Every step forward is a win."
"Progress is more important than perfection."
"I believe in my ability to improve."

___
___
___
___
___

Step 7: Reward Yourself

What small reward can you give yourself for reaching each milestone?
Example: "After running 2 miles, I'll treat myself to a smoothie."

___
___

What will your big reward be once you accomplish your main goal?
Example: "After completing the 5K, I'll buy myself new running shoes."

___
___

References

1 Duckworth AL, Peterson C, Matthews MD, Kelly DR. Grit: perseverance and passion for long-term goals. *J Pers Soc Psychol*. 2007;92(6):1087.
2 Duckworth AL, Eskreis-Winkler L. Grit. In: Wright JD, editor. *International encyclopedia of the social & behavioral sciences*. 2nd ed. Oxford: Elsevier; 2015. p. 397–401.
3 Urgo K, Arguello J. The effects of goal-setting on learning outcomes and self-regulated learning processes. In: Proceedings of the 2024 *conference* on Human Information Interaction and Retrieval, Sheffield, United Kingdom. 2024 Mar; p. 278–290.
4 Wang H, Wang S, Tlili A, Li M, Yang D, Adarkwah MA, et al. The combined effects of goal attributes, motivational beliefs, creativity and grit on self-regulation in online ill-structured problem solving: a fsQCA approach. BMC Psychol. 2025;13(1):27.
5 Billore S, Anisimova T, Vrontis D. Self-regulation and goal-directed behavior: a systematic literature review, public policy recommendations, and research agenda. *J Bus Res*. 2023;156:113435.
6 Prochaska JO, DiClemente CC. Stages and processes of self-change of smoking: toward an integrative model of change. *J Consult Clin Psychol*. 1983;51(3):390–395.

11 The Role of Families and Society in Making Progress toward a Successful Launch

The Role of the Parents/Caretakers and the Family System

When you are a child, the role of a parent or main support person is to provide a close hands-on approach. As a child learns to walk, parents will hold their hands up as they encourage them to take their first steps. This helps a child build confidence while at the same time trusting that the parent will always be by their side. For most parents, it is instinctual to be by their child's side guiding them to make the best choice possible as they advance through life's challenges. Ultimately, the role of the parent is to prepare their child to be an independent and self-sufficient adult. It is to essentially prepare the child enough to let them go and take the reins of life themselves.

Depending on a parent or caretaker's own personal set of values and personality, the parenting style will fall within the following four categories: permissive, neglectful, authoritative, and authoritarian.[1] What are these types of parenting and how do they potentially impact you or your child's growth? Some parenting styles make it harder for children to eventually become independent, while others set them up for a successful transition into adulthood.

For example, a type of parenting called "permissive" is when a child is allowed to make most of their own decisions. Despite being a child themselves, the parents allow them (or give them permission) to parent themselves. For example, a child could be allowed to decide what they eat for dinner every night, or when they will go to bed, or when and how much homework they will do. Discipline is used sparingly, if ever, and if the child does experience any challenges in their life, the parent steps in to provide relief in any capacity they can. The parent typically engages with their child in a warm and calm manner.

Another parenting style is called "neglectful." In this parenting style, the child's basic needs (e.g., water, food, shelter) may be met (but not always); however, the parent does not attend to the emotions of the child. Unlike the permissive parent, they do not present as warm and comforting, but more ignoring and unaffected. Though, like the permissive parent, they will

DOI: 10.4324/9781003649410-11

provide few structures or limitations to guide the child to success. It is up to the child themselves to provide these frameworks and structures for success.

The "authoritarian" parent expresses high expectations of the child and with a strict, rigid approach. This parenting style includes the frequent use of punishment to shape a child's behavior. Finally, the most optimal and healthy style of parenting is what is called the "authoritative" style. This style is where the parenting network clearly communicates expectations with consequences while maintaining a warm, trusting relationship. This parenting style also highlights flexibility although the parent is clearly the decision-maker. The authoritative parenting style is viewed as the most supportive style of a child's social emotional development with children most likely to feel confident and self-motivated.

As a child transitions to adolescence and into young adulthood, the parenting role should ideally adapt to promote continued development of age-appropriate independent skills. According to Stixrud and Johnson[2], as a child moves into young adulthood, parents are encouraged to transition from the "manager" to "consultant" role to promote confidence in decision-making and promote self-efficacy. A "manager" parent is one who feels a high sense of responsibility for the child's success and quickly jumps in to fix their problems. However, the "consultant/advisor" parent offers help and advice that encourages independent skills development. This style allows the child to make better connections between their choices (e.g., should I study an extra 30 minutes or play video games?) and the natural consequence (e.g., performing poorly on a test due to inadequate study time). The transition from "manager" to "consultant" is particularly helpful during the teen years as the focus becomes more on supporting a child to increase their competence in managing life responsibilities versus handling it for them.

Worksheet: Determining Parenting Style

Answer the questions below to see what type of parenting style you may institute as a parent/caregiver or experienced as a teen/emerging young adult. Reflect on the three following parenting style categories that are a combination of the traditional list of parenting styles along with the updated concept of *manager* vs. *consultant.*

Permissive Parenting/the "Friend"

A Is there a struggle with setting boundaries (e.g., curfew, chores) or expressing expectations regarding academic performance because it may cause conflict in your relationship?
B Are excuses made for any lack of progress on the teen/young adult's part? Does the parent/caregiver allow for missed responsibilities or shield the teen/young adult from natural consequences? Does the teen/young adult

not know how to experience a negative consequence and move through it effectively?

C Is the relationship between the support system/parent and the teen/young adult reciprocal (i.e., do you both give as much as you get, or is one party giving/receiving more than the other)?

Authoritarian Parenting/the "Manager"

A Are there clear boundaries in the relationship between the parent/support system and the teen/young adult? Or is the parent using language such as "because I said so" 90% of the time?

B When the teen/young adult struggles with life (e.g., academics or sports), does the parent internalize these feelings of disappointment and shame? Is the parent quick to intervene to increase their child's success?

C Is the parent more focused on their teen/young adults' success rather than their personal growth trajectory?

Authoritative Parenting/the "Consultant" Advisor

A When a teen/young adult is facing a challenge, are they provided emotional support and guidance as they do most of the work or does the parent/support system step in and do the work for them?

B When there is conflict with the teen/young adult, is the goal to "win" the argument or to understand one another's perspective to make a more supportive and informed decision?

C Are there at least three chores or other tasks that the teen/young adult can manage on their own and be responsible for independently implementing?

D Is the teen/young adult allowed to experience natural consequences or does the parent/support system protect them?

Parents can take an active role in supporting their child to feel confident and have the appropriate skills to thrive in young adulthood by stepping back and allowing them to work through challenges. The teen/young adult should take an active role in their own independent skills development in collaboration with their parents. As parents are advised to shift their role from *manager*—directly dictating daily schedule and tasks, to *consultant*—providing advice and guidance as needed and/or requested, the emerging young adult should shift from seeking structure and approval from the parents to seeking advice on specific issues. This practice will help in supporting the transition to young adulthood and decrease the likelihood of the young adult's overreliance on the parents for decision-making.[3-5] Think of parents as being those teachers/mentors who are your consultants in life but are not responsible for implementing every step that will make it successful.

We do not learn to competently drive a car by reading about it, watching it online or via a video game, we must practice adult responsibilities that are developmentally appropriate at each age. We must get a feel for what it means to organize, plan, and implement life skills by practicing daily and working through the expected challenges. For parents/caregivers, having your child practice basic life skills while they are still home with you is the best way to provide guidance and assist with problem-solving challenges.

Designation of Responsibilities

Child developmental studies have found that when children regularly participate in household chores, they develop a sense of self-competence, prosocial behaviors, and even improved academic performance.[6] Furthermore, children who participated in household chores at an earlier age were more likely to achieve career success as young adults compared to those who did not have chores or who just started them as teens.[7] Not only do age-appropriate chores help with developing self-competence and academic/professional success, but they are also positively associated with successfully adapting to college/post high-school life, as students feel more confident in managing multiple responsibilities independently.[8]

Since this book is focused on supporting teens/young adults successfully transitioning to independence, let us again review the types of age-appropriate chores we covered in depth in Chapter 4. Household chores for a teen/emerging young adult should start with foundational skills and move toward full independence. During your teen years, it is appropriate to learn to follow multistep instructions for tasks that include planning and execution. Furthermore, this is an opportunity to practice overseeing a task with minimal reminders from your parents/support system. In many ways, chores are a practice run for the real world, especially when you are living independently, and parents are not providing reminders.

Below is a chart of extended chores for teens aged 13–18 years, separated by early adolescence to late adolescence aiming at scaffolding skills (building on previous ones) based on developmental stage. This chart covers some of the same, but also additional chores from Chapter 4.

Chore category	*Ages 13–15 (foundational)*	*Ages 16–18 (independence)*
Kitchen	Dishwasher management, cook one basic family dinner/week	Full dinner planning and prep, grocery shopping (from list)
General house cleaning	Deep clean personal bedroom/bathroom, vacuum/mop entire floor	Detailed maintenance of shared spaces

Chore category	*Ages 13–15 (foundational)*	*Ages 16–18 (independence)*
Laundry	Do all personal laundry	Manage household linens/towels
Home/auto	Mow lawn/basic yardwork	Basic car maintenance (wash/ oil check) and minor home maintenance
Adult prep	Manage school schedule/ deadlines	Manage personal budget/ bank, make medical/dentist appointments

Participation in chores does not just help the household function better, but it also brings family members together as a community and fosters a sense of self-efficacy for the teen/young adult. Again, the concept of self-efficacy is the belief in one's ability to implement strategies independently to achieve a goal. Self-efficacy helps in preventing learned helplessness, which is when a teen/young adult faced with repeated stressors eventually stops attempting to change their situation even if they have the skills to change it. Learned helplessness is often seen in young adults who struggle with successfully transitioning to independence or who fail to launch. The research on the positive association between chores and academic/professional success highlights the benefits of learning to manage time and personal obligations to offset the development of learned helplessness and its negative effects.[4]

Aside from participating in household chores, learning how to navigate the stress of failure can also contribute to self-efficacy. Parents/support systems can support their teen/young adult in managing the stress of failure by seeing them as opportunities for learning that will help with future success. If you live in a city, this will mean teaching a teen to take public transportation to school or to a shopping center on their own. If at some point they miss their stop or get lost, parents/support systems can provide guidance as the "consultant" and suggest ways to problem solve in the moment vs. swooping in to save them from the experience altogether. If a teen has a major school project and is involved in a demanding sport, a parent/support system could advise them on which one to prioritize but then step back and allow them to make the choice.

Parents/support systems can lead by example in how they cope with their child's failures as well as their own. If parents react to their own or their teen/young adult's failure with anxiety or pity, parents might instill learned helplessness.[9] According to the researchers, when parents model a "failure is actually enhancing" mindset, a failure becomes a data point for future development versus a truly devastating loss. Teens/young adults are then more likely to develop an internal locus of control or the belief that one's actions directly determine outcomes. Children adopt the same self-talk as their parents when managing failure.[10] When parents use language to model failure as external, specific and temporary, they are role modeling strategies to cope with learned helplessness and offer a way to cope with failure with resilience. Parents/support givers—next time you are faced with a challenge in the presence of your teen/young adult (e.g., struggling with putting furniture together, burning breakfast, or not getting a promotion), take the opportunity to role model coping through failure. Tell your teen/young adult your experience and what you did to handle the situation, your thoughts, and emotions.

Based on the discussion of parenting styles above, we know that the authoritative style and consultant parent best supports the teen/young adult in developing the skills needed to increase feelings of self-efficacy and confidence in managing the demands of independent adult life. A parent who uses a permissive style that overaccommodates, does not communicate clear expectations, and hesitates in setting boundaries has a higher likelihood of fostering learned helplessness resulting in *failure to launch*. For example, repeated avoidance of expressing expectations about homework compliance when observing struggles with academic performance will communicate to the teen/young adult a lack of responsibility over their behaviors (except when there is an undiagnosed learning disability). Teens who have little demands placed on them since childhood will have difficulty when their parents begin to express expectations and try to set limits. They might begin to challenge the demands, become dysregulated, and withdraw. This reinforces the permissive parent's assumption that their child/young adult will experience intolerable distress if they place any demands on them. This results in a cycle of reinforcement for both parents and the teen/young adult (Figure 11.1).

Behavioral Cycle of Reinforcement

Family-Based Treatment

Although the aim of this book is to assist parents/support systems and teens/young adults in *preventing failure to launch*, there are already evidence-based interventions that target decrease in parental overaccommodation and increase in self-efficacy for young adults who *currently* struggle with independence (i.e., those who currently have NOT launched successfully). The aim of these behavioral interventions is to break the cycle of reinforcement that is related to *failure to launch*. Berger and Lebowitz created a Failure to Launch (FTL) adaptation of the Supportive Parenting for Anxious Childhood Emotions (SPACE treatment program) and identified five key treatment components: reducing parental accommodation, increasing parental support, de-escalation, and engaging supporters.[11,12]

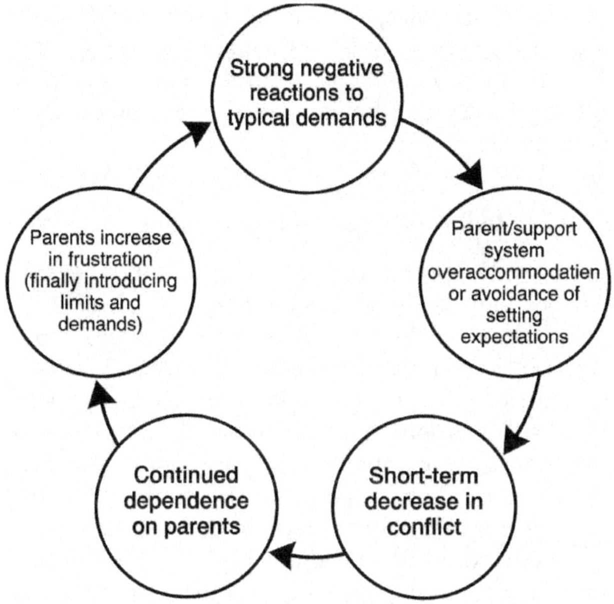

Figure 11.1 A circular flow diagram shows a repeating cycle: strong negative reactions to typical demands lead to parents or support systems over accommodating or avoiding expectations, resulting in a short-term decrease in conflict, which leads to continued dependence on parents, and eventually increased parental frustration when limits are introduced, restarting the cycle.

These components are adapted to best fit the developmental expectations of the young adult patient to engage in independent behavior while supporting parents with clear boundaries and expectations via written announcements applied in a gradual manner. SPACE–FTL[11,12] is specifically targeted to work with the parents without the involvement of the young adult in the sessions as it focuses on changing the parents overaccommodating style. Another family-based approach to *failure to launch* would be family therapy in which the struggling young adult and parents are both active in the treatment to address family dynamics that reinforce the *failure to launch* behavior in the young adult.[13–15]

Remember that our program is a *preventative* model, and so we not only expect, but we encourage the involvement of your parent/support system in the process of developing as an independent and functional young adult. It is only when someone has already reached the *clinical stage* of *failing to launch* that they need to be significantly weaned off their parental support system. However, as we discussed above, it is important that a family work as a team in our process, changing their involvement and their roles as their child progresses from younger developmental ages/stages to that of a young adult; transitioning the parental role from *manager* to *consultant*. We all need supports in place before they are taken away and we can stand alone and upright on our own two feet.

The Role of Social Media and Societal Expectations

Social media opened opportunities to foster social connections with people we see in our daily lives and expand our social network with communities around the world. Where before societal values and expectations were limited to our local community and our exposure to role models on TV shows and movies, now we are exposed to a wide range of values that shift quickly based on trends. For emerging young adults, this developmental period includes continued identity formation and the pressure to make decisions about careers, relationships, and financial independence. Social media can serve as a source of information about what others in the same age group are exploring and coping with in the transition to young adulthood. Unfortunately, social media is a place that can set unrealistic expectations about success in young adulthood.

Social media can increase stress as young adults are exposed to carefully curated and idealized milestone content from influencers regarding homeownership, relationships, high-paying jobs or luxury travel. This creates perceived pressure to conform to an unrealistic timeline for a typical emerging young adult.[16] Visual platforms, which encourage curated and idealized images (Instagram, Tik Tok), were more associated with negative emotions related to feeling greater pressure and upward comparison. This could lead to feelings of inadequacy and learned helplessness due to repeated exposure to stressors that feel outside an emerging young adult's control.[16] With exposure to these unrealistic timelines, young adults are placing pressure on themselves to seek out promotions and higher salaries within months of starting an entry-level position. These accelerated career expectations influenced by social media's "hustle culture" or "passive income" content can lead to young adults being biased against entry-level roles that do not facilitate the high-status lifestyles they see online. By hesitating to take on entry-level roles, they might turn down employment opportunities and increase the risk of *failure to launch*. We would like to think we are exceptions to the rule (e.g., I will be a social media star with billions of followers), but more times than not, we are often the rule. So, setting realistic expectations is of the utmost importance.

Although the risks of social media's influence on social expectations of independent young adults are well-documented, there are benefits to social media in helping young adults increase career self-efficacy, access social support and increase skills acquisition. One study found that for college students, social media users had more employment options than those who did not use social media.[17] Students who were actively engaged in social media to gather information on potential employers find these efforts facilitate recruitment opportunities that better align with their work values. Also, these students are more aware of the impression their social media presence could have on potential employers and are more engaged in their corporate impression management. They are more likely to foster a professional support network through connecting with alumni, career experts, and professional online communities to better inform them in their employment decisions. By being more actively engaged in the employment process from recruitment to interview and job acceptance, the young adult experiences a high degree of self-efficacy and can even feel more successful.

Young adults who can successfully obtain stable employment through their own research of potential employers and establishing a professional support network demonstrate qualities that are the antithesis (opposite) to helplessness. Social media can also be a platform for those who are motivated to seek information for skills acquisition to support their adult independence. Via social media, young adults can access helpful information on financial literacy (e.g., filing taxes, budgeting), cooking and positive health behaviors.[18] It is developmentally appropriate for emerging adults to seek consultation with others outside of their families and it reinforces a sense of self-confidence/efficacy in taking the initiative to actively engage in problem solving without relying on parents/caregivers to identify the solution for them.

There are strategies that are helpful for weeding out the harmful, unhelpful social media content regarding social expectations and focusing more on accurate educational content. The research suggests that strategies should focus on learning how to recognize "curated" unrealistic content via enhancing digital literacy, having mindful consumption through resisting "doom scrolling," and using the information learned to help with goal setting that matches their current resources.[18]

Worksheet: Learning How to Pick Out Helpful Information in Social Media

We are naturally pulled toward visual images that invoke strong emotions whether positive or negative. The following are a list of questions to consider as you scroll through your social media feed.

A Does the room featured in the post look lived-in, or does it lack evidence of someone living there such as cords, clutter etc.? If it looks like a showroom, then it is likely a room that has been staged for the post.

B What is NOT in the frame of the posted photo? Is it limited to a section of the room, then it is likely that clutter is present just outside the frame.
C Is there a featured product in the post such as a specific brand or a luxury product? If there is, then there is a good possibility that the content creator will receive the product for free or is being paid by the secret sponsor.
D Are you comparing an intentionally curated 15-second vacation video reel to your 24-hour daily life? There are likely significant hidden costs associated with their luxurious lifestyle. You do not know if they have resources available to them of which you are unaware (e.g., family money).
E Does the creator only talk about their successes and not failures? If you only see the creator posting success that seems to be obtained with minimal effort, then they are sharing only part of the process.
F How does viewing the content make you feel? Does it inspire motivation? Notice if it instead makes you feel inadequate.
G Question why the content was posted. Was it for educational purposes or for performative reasons to increase views and likes for the creator's own financial gain?

Conclusion

In summary, this chapter identified the role that parents and their teens/young adults can take to increase the skills and self-efficacy needed to successfully transition into independent adulthood. Parents who demonstrated a more authoritative style and were able to shift from the *manager* to *consultant* role helped their teens/young adults gain a greater sense of control and confidence in their ability to manage situations while still having the guidance of their parents/support system. Parents/caregivers who took a step back in a supportive manner and allowed their teens/young adults to learn from their failures set up their emerging young adults for greater success. Teens/young adults who take a more active role not only with household tasks but also with engaging with their social network were more likely to experience success with their academics and career goals. While adapting to shifts in the parent-child relationship can be challenging for both parents/caregivers and teens/young adults, maintaining flexibility is key to fostering autonomy and independence and preventing *failure to launch*.

References

1 Levin E. Baumrind's parenting styles. In: Goldstein S, Naglieri JA, editors. *Encyclopedia of child behavior and development*. Boston (MA): Springer; 2011.

2 Stixrud WR, Johnson N. The self-driven child: the science and sense of giving your kids more control over their lives. New York (NY): Viking; 2018.
3 Arnett JJ, Fishel E. Getting to 30: a parent's guide to the 20-somethings. New York (NY): Workman Publishing; 2024.
4 Fingerman KL, Cheng YP, Wesselmann ED, Zarit S, Furstenberg FF, Birditt KS. Helicopter parents and landing pad kids: intense parental support of grown children. *J Marriage Fam*. 2012;74(4):880–896.
5 Myers SA, Glover NP. Emerging adults' use of relational maintenance behaviors with their parents. *Commun Res Rep*. 2007;24(3):257–264.
6 White EM, DeBoer MD, Scharf RJ. Associations between household chores and childhood self-competency. *J Dev Behav Pediatr*. 2019;40(3):176–182.
7 Rossmann MM. *Involving children in household tasks: is it worth the effort?* St. Paul (MN): University of Minnesota Extension Service; 2002 Sep.
8 Lythcott-Haims J. How to raise an adult: break free of the overparenting trap and prepare your kid for success. New York (NY): Henry Holt and Company; 2015.
9 Haimovitz K, Dweck CS. What predicts children's fixed and growth mindsets? Not their parents' views of intelligence but their parents' views of failure. *Psychol Sci*. 2016;27(6):859–869.
10 Maier SF, Seligman MEP. Learned helplessness at fifty: insights from neuroscience. *Psychol Rev*. 2016;123(4):349–367.
11 Berger U, Lebowitz ER. Parent training for dependent, yet abled, young adults. *Bull Menninger Clin*. 2022 Summer;86(3):249–281.
12 Lebowitz ER, Omer H, Hermes H, Scahill L. Parent training for childhood anxiety disorders: the SPACE program. *J Clin Child Adolesc Psychol*. 2014;43(3):456–469.
13 Carter EA, McGoldrick M, editors. The expanded family life cycle: individual, family, and social perspectives. 5th ed. Boston (MA): Pearson; 2015.
14 Minuchin S. Families and family therapy. Cambridge (MA): Harvard University Press; 1974.
15 Nichols MP, Davis SD. Family therapy: concepts and methods. 11th ed. Boston (MA): Pearson; 2020.
16 O'Connell R, Daruwala NA. Milestones and mindsets: how social media shapes young adults' expectations and emotional well-being. *J Soc Media Res*. 2025;2(5):400–415.
17 Li F, Shi M, Feng R. Social media use and job choices: the mediating roles of work values and self-efficacy. *Front Psychol*. 2025;16:1485663.
18 Friedman VJ, Wright CJC, Molenaar A, McCaffrey T, Brennan L, Lim MSC. The use of social media as a persuasive platform to facilitate nutrition and health behavior change in young adults: web-based conversation study. *J Med Internet Res*. 2022;24(5):1–15.

12 Clinical Disorders and Their Contribution to Failure to Launch

There are several disorders that contribute to *failure to launch*. This chapter will introduce clinical psychological disorders as well as areas of clinical concern that increase the risk of developing *failure to launch* in young adults. As highlighted in previous chapters, there are a variety of societal and familial factors that contribute to the risk of *failure to launch*, and having a psychological disorder or other clinical concerns can further increase the risk. While reviewing clinical psychological disorders in this chapter, there will be frequent references to a diagnostic manual used by mental health professionals called the Diagnostic and Statistical Manual of Mental Disorders, 5th edition text revision (DSM-5-TR), considered the "diagnostic bible" of mental health disorders. Researchers and clinicians have made several revisions of this diagnostic manual over the past several decades as they discover new information about mental health disorders. The classifications in this manual are recognized by the medical community as comparable to any other medical diagnosis.

Although the teen and young adult years are filled with positive emotional experiences, expected stressors and rapid development during this critical time can also bring way to intense negative emotions. Some of these negative emotions are normal and expected reactions to stressors such as feeling nervous waiting for college acceptance or feeling disappointed for not making it on the varsity team. For others in this age group, negative emotions can be significantly distressing and get in the way of daily life. When negative emotions are persistent and *interfere* with daily living, a clinical disorder may be present.

For those diagnosed with a clinical disorder, approximately 50% develop at least one by age 14 and 75% by 24 years of age.[1] When studying age groups for the rate of clinical psychological disorders, young adults were found to have the highest rates. Overall, 36.2% of U.S. young adults between the ages of 18–25 experience a clinical disorder.[2] This population is at very high risk of developing difficulties with successfully transitioning to independence due to dealing with these stressors.

DOI: 10.4324/9781003649410-12

Anxiety and Depressive Disorders

The notion of anxiety can frequently be confused with experiencing an actual, diagnosable anxiety disorder. Anxiety is a normal emotional reaction to a potential threat and can be a helpful emotion. If we did not experience anxiety, such as worrying about a potential negative consequence, we would not pay our bills on time or we would miss our plane. When an anxiety disorder is present, worry or fear gets in the way of our daily functioning (e.g., in work, school, family/friends). In fact, anxiety disorders are one of the most common clinical disorders in 18–29-year-olds, with research showing it is found in approximately 1 in 5 young adults.[3] There are a variety of specific anxiety disorders that fall under this category. Since the focus of this book is on *failure to launch*, we will focus on the specific anxiety disorders that are seen more commonly among this group. We provide an overview of the following anxiety disorders: obsessive-compulsive disorder, social anxiety disorder, panic disorder (with/without agoraphobia), specific phobia, and generalized anxiety disorder.

Obsessive-Compulsive Disorder

Most people commonly associate obsessive-compulsive disorder (OCD) with someone who worries about germs and excessively handwashes or someone who is highly organized. In fact, OCD includes a wide range of themes related to obsessions, intrusive thoughts, along with compulsive behaviors. Approximately 1.5% of the young adults between 18 and 29 in the United States have been diagnosed with OCD.[1] Overall, the lifetime prevalence for all adults is 2.3%.[1]

The following are common themes found in OCD:

1 Obsessions

- Fear of germs and disease
- Fear that you might be responsible for something bad happening
- Fear of acting impulsively
- Fear of making the wrong decision/making a mistake
- Developing a deadly disease

2 Compulsions

- Excessive handwashing
- The need to do a behavior until it's "just right"
- Research online regarding health symptoms
- Seeking repeated reassurance from friends and family
- Engaging in repetitive behaviors (checking stove multiple times, turning light switches off and on)

These intrusive thoughts and behaviors can significantly get in the way of daily tasks such as getting ready for school in the morning or completing a school assignment on time. They can also cause tension in social relationships when a person is engaged in repeated reassurance seeking or insists that others also participate in the compulsion (e.g., also keep the house immaculately clean). Young adults who are at risk of *failure to launch* may struggle to effectively manage these thoughts and behaviors, which result in them not being able to attend school or work.

Social Anxiety Disorder

An anxiety disorder that is quite common among young adults is social anxiety disorder. Social anxiety disorder affects about 9.1% of U.S. young adults.[1] Social anxiety disorder is more than just being shy and is sometimes confused with being "introverted." To clarify, an introverted person is someone who prefers to get their emotional energy from within with preferences to engage in minimally social stimulating environments. Introverts do not necessarily experience anxiety around social interactions; it just takes more of their energy to engage in a highly stimulating social situation.

However, *clinical* social anxiety includes the following symptoms:

a Significant nervousness or fear in social situations
b Excessive fear of negative social judgment, embarrassment, or being rejected.
c The presence of distressing physical anxiety symptoms when in social situations (e.g., blushing, sweating, trembling).
d The above symptoms interfere with accomplishing daily living tasks (e.g., making a presentation at school or work).

Social anxiety may greatly interfere with initiating and maintaining friendships and self-advocating at school or on the job. More severe forms may interfere with the ability to interact with anyone outside of a few select people. Sometimes very socially anxious teens and young adults might even struggle interacting with extended family. Social anxiety might be experienced along with intense physical anxiety symptoms including rapid heart rate, tension, or nausea. For an emerging young adult, this type of anxiety can significantly limit their ability to engage with the world beyond their family, especially since independent adulthood depends on interacting with others to manage everyday responsibilities. These may include applying for jobs, communicating with a landlord about apartment repairs, or advocating for themselves in academic or workplace settings.

Panic Disorder

Panic disorder is the fear of suddenly experiencing intense physical symptoms of anxiety that appear "out of the blue" and are perceived as distressing in and of themselves.

Other symptoms of panic disorder include:

a Intense physical symptoms such as racing heart, dizziness, shakiness, sweating, nausea, feeling weak, lightheadedness, derealization.
b Fear of losing control with urges to escape.
c Intense symptoms typically last no longer than ten minutes.
d Following a panic attack, there is at least one month of fear that another panic attack will occur.
e There is no other medical condition or substance responsible for this sudden onset of symptoms.

For young adults in the United States, approximately 2.8% report experiencing full-blown panic disorder.[1] For many people who fear panic attacks, they also fear being in situations where they could have a panic attack and feel it would be difficult to escape. These include enclosed or crowded places such as concerts or grocery stores. Sometimes people with panic attacks may fear open spaces as they might experience sensations (e.g., derealization) that could trigger their panic attacks. The fear of places that are difficult to escape is referred to as agoraphobia and can accompany panic disorder but can also occur without. Living with the fear of an unexpected panic attack and engaging in avoidant behaviors can be all consuming and limit a person's ability to leave their home to attend school/work. Even with current access to online shopping, bill paying, and remote school/work, a person with a constant fear of panic paired with fear of being outside of the safety of their home would result in an extremely limited and closed off life. A young adult could become at risk of *failure to launch* with this clinical disorder.

Specific Phobia

Specific phobia refers to a fearful response to a trigger as well as anticipatory anxiety at the possibility of being exposed to the specific trigger. There are a wide range of phobias that can be put into four major categories: natural environment, animals, medical treatment/blood injection-injury, and situational. Specific examples of phobias include fear of dogs, thunderstorms, vaccines and blood draws, and fear of flying.

When in these fearful situations, people experience intense distress, often accompanied by panic attacks. Phobias are highly distressing and often get in the way of daily functioning. For example, a person with a phobia associated with blood draws/vaccines might make concerted efforts to avoid these procedures, including avoiding medical visits even when they have an issue requiring evaluation. Another example is phobia related to vomit called emetophobia. Those with emetophobia have an intense fear of vomiting or being in the presence of vomiting that often interferes with being around others or situations where there is a possibility (albeit remote) of vomiting. They might even avoid certain foods for fear of food poisoning that might result in vomiting. The list of specific phobias can be endless and is not limited to what we have discussed in this chapter. If an emerging young adult has a strong specific phobia (e.g., fear of flying) and their job requires them to get on an airplane, they would be at risk of inadequately performing on the job and getting fired.

Generalized Anxiety Disorder (GAD)

In the United States, 2.0% of young adults between 18 and 29 years old report experiencing anxiety symptoms that meet the criteria for GAD.[1] For teens in the United States, about 2.2% have GAD, which could interfere with their ability to attend school in a consistent manner given the excessive worry and physical symptoms associated with GAD.[1]

The clinical diagnosis of GAD includes experiencing the following anxiety symptoms:

a Excessive and uncontrollable worry
b Restlessness
c Muscle tension (back pain, headaches)
d "Feeling on edge"
e Difficulty concentrating
f Difficulty with sleep
g Irritability

The overwhelming worry could be related to a variety of themes such as academic performance or worries about the future. These symptoms are experienced every day, nearly all day for a period of at least six months. This is different from experiencing brief, situational anxiety that improves once the situation has resolved, such as waiting for the results of an exam. GAD is more persistent and significantly interferes with daily activities including your sleep. When a person with GAD is asked the question "Does worry control you or do you control worry?" the person with GAD will typically respond that the worry controls them. A young adult with GAD would struggle to succeed across many domains of adult independence (e.g., relationships, personal health maintenance, job performance) if anxiety is frequently and overwhelmingly invading their life.

Major Depression

Clinical depression is different from situational sadness and low mood. It is normal to feel moments of sadness in reaction to the death of a loved one or when a goal we tried so hard to work toward is not achieved. However, clinical depression, or major depressive disorder, signifies a more persistent low mood and several of the following:

a Loss of pleasure in activities that were once enjoyable (anhedonia)
b Irritability
c Low Energy
d Restlessness or moving slowly
e Difficulty with concentration
f Insomnia or excessive sleep
g Notable changes in weight
h Changes in appetite
i Worthlessness
j Hopelessness
k Suicidal thoughts and behaviors

For major depressive disorders, symptoms are present for at least two weeks almost all day, nearly every day. Additionally, depression symptoms are seen as significantly interfering with important activities such as attending school/work and keeping up relationships with friends and family. Severe symptoms can even interfere with basic activities of daily life such as eating, personal hygiene, and other basic self-care activities. In the United States, approximately 18.6% of young adults ages 18–25 reported experiencing levels of depression that meet criteria for a major depressive disorder episode in the past 12 months.[2] For teens in the United States, approximately 20.1% report experiencing depression in the past year, which signifies an estimated 3.7 million.[2] For this age group, sadness might not be observed as the most prominent symptom, but rather an *irritable* mood that is also present with the symptoms above.

Bipolar Disorder

Another mood disorder that is present in the DSM-V-TR and that has a combination of low, depressed mood along with episodes of elevated manic symptoms is called bipolar disorder. Bipolar disorder is different from major depression in that the person experiences episodes of elevated mood that are different from their typical mood and are causing significant difficulties and disruptions in their lives.

Manic symptoms include the following:

a Intense euphoria
b High irritability
c Grandiosity
d Risk behaviors (impulsive behaviors that are dangerous such as driving while intoxicated, sexual promiscuity)
e Pressured speech
f Racing thoughts
g Little to no sleep coupled with increased energy
h Might include psychotic symptoms (breaks from reality such as the belief that they have "superpowers")

There are two types of manic episodes: hypomania and mania. Hypomania includes most of the above symptoms, but the severity is not as intense, and the person does not require inpatient hospitalization. Furthermore, the person with hypomania must experience symptoms for at least four consecutive days for most of the day. A person who is manic exhibits most of the symptoms described above with greater severity and impact on their daily functioning. Additionally, to qualify for mania a person must exhibit these symptoms for seven consecutive days, and the severity must be severe enough to require inpatient hospitalization. In addition to episodes of manic or hypomanic symptoms, the person will also experience episodes of major depression. Bipolar disorder is considered a chronic, lifelong condition that responds very well to a combination of medication and cognitive behavioral treatments. The key is adhering to the treatment recommendations on a consistent basis. A major barrier to this population thriving independently as young adults is treatment adherence.

Executive Functioning and Learning Concerns

There are a wide range of neurodevelopmental disorders that could also contribute to the risk of *failure to launch*. Neurodevelopmental disorders are recognized as starting in childhood. In this next section, we will focus on specific types of neurodevelopmental disorders that are not associated with intellectual disability but still might cause impairments in daily functioning. Although these disorders are typically considered life long, there are excellent evidence-based interventions that can help teens and young adults learn to manage these challenges.

Attention-Deficit Hyperactivity Disorder (ADHD)

To begin, we want to establish that there is no formal diagnosis of "ADD." The formal clinical diagnosis is called "ADHD" and then it is categorized into one of three subtypes: inattentive, hyperactive/impulsive, or combination of these two. About 7 million or 11.4% of U.S. children and teens have been diagnosed with ADHD.[4] A common misconception of ADHD is that a person is unable to sustain their attention to a given task. In essence, ADHD is difficulty regulating attention and shifting flexibly to another task that might be of perceived low interest. Parents might observe a teen suspected of having ADHD intensely focusing on certain high-interest activities or themes.

Symptoms associated with ADHD by subcategory include the following:

I Hyperactivity and impulsivity:

  a Often fidgets with or taps hands or feet.
  b Often leaves their seat in situations when remaining seated is expected.
  c Often runs or climbs in situations where it is inappropriate.
  d Often "on the go."
  e Often talks excessively and is impulsive.
  f Often interrupts or intrudes on others; for teens-they may intrude into or take over what others are doing.

II Inattention:

  a Often fails to give close attention to details or make careless mistakes.
  b Often has difficulties sustaining attention.
  c Often does not seem to listen when spoken to directly.
  d Often does not follow through on instructions and fails to finish schoolwork, chores, or tasks at work.
  e Often avoids, dislikes, or is reluctant to engage in tasks that require sustained effort.
  f Often has difficulty organizing tasks and activities.
  g Often is forgetful with daily activities.

These symptoms are typically observed in a variety of settings including home and school/work. ADHD is a disorder of executive functioning that affects different areas of life, not just academic and work performance.[5] In this population, deficits are observed in self-awareness, inhibition, nonverbal working memory, verbal working memory, emotional self-regulation, self-motivation, and planning/problem solving. These skills are necessary for life functioning, including on the spot effective problem solving, such as when life throws you a curve ball (e.g., car battery dies) or engaging in a task when there is no immediate consequence (e.g., doing laundry on a regular basis). ADHD can present challenges for teens and young adults in both their academic and personal life. Challenges with self-directed planning, organization, and follow-through can make it harder to complete homework, prepare for exams, keep medical appointments, sustain social relationships, and arrive at work on time. ADHD can affect social relationships by contributing to impulsive behavior in conversations with friends, delays in responding to text messages, missed social commitments, and difficulty managing emotions during interpersonal conflict.

Let us provide you an example here of *failure to launch* with the abovementioned clinical concerns. A 25-year-old presented to therapy requesting their psychologist pressure their parents into stepping back from pushing them toward acquiring employment. The young adult reported a history of ADHD (combined type). Three years ago, they graduated from college with the minimal GPA and requirements to receive a BA in philosophy. Since college, they had been residing in their childhood home and had been financially supported by their parents. Their parents paid for their groceries, phone bill, gym memberships, and they lived rent free. They believed they had completed all present and future obligations by graduating college. They had no plans for the future, did not want to plan for the future, and wanted their parents to "be quiet, back off, and continue to support them." Their parents were very frustrated and expressed wanting to "cut them off" but were unwilling to do so unless their child first searched and secured employment, of which their child had no intention. The young adult had also never learned goal planning and follow through/completion. In college, they had over-relied on educational accommodations and had not developed and practiced compensatory strategies.

As you may be able to see in this example, clinical diagnoses (e.g., ADHD), with lack of skills acquisition, goal planning, and family dynamics contributed to actual *failure to launch*. It is never just one diagnosis or one disagreement with a family member that leads to dysfunction. This example underlies how important it is to learn skills and to have several experiences of trial and error over time to become a successful, independent young adult.

ADHD is a clinical disorder that can also be further complicated by co-occurring anxiety, depression, and learning disabilities. The 2007 National Survey of Children's Health found that 33% of children with ADHD also met criteria for another disorder.[6] The most common disorder found to be co-occurring with ADHD is a learning disorder (45%).[1] In the next section, a brief overview of the main learning disorders will be presented.

Learning Disorders

According to DSM-5-TR, there are specific learning disorders that start in childhood and specifically affect the learning process in the following domains: reading, writing, spelling, and understanding mathematical concepts. These learning difficulties must last at least six months even after targeted educational interventions. According to research, data shows that the prevalence of learning disorders in the general U.S. population is anywhere between 5% and 9%.[7] The following are specific learning disorders recognized in the DSM-5-TR: impairments in reading, written expression, and mathematics. These disorders are commonly recognized as dyslexia (reading), dysgraphia (writing), and dyscalculia (math). For these learning disorders, one of the core features is that these difficulties are observed in elementary school with the introduction of academic work. They also might not be readily apparent until the later school years when academic demands increase. For children and teens who are suspected of having a learning disorder, they must demonstrate significant challenges with learning key academic skills. Additionally, these learning challenges must be seen as "well below" than "expected" for the child's age and development and cause significant difficulties with academic performance. An example for a young elementary school aged child would be significant and persistent difficulties with single word pronunciation and fluency that would indicate some difficulties with reading. This would result in them not being able to expand their reading skills, thus missing out on key concepts in later school years. For a teen who struggles with written expression, they might have shown persistent difficulties with spelling, grammar, and punctuation. As you might imagine, if a junior in high school is struggling with successfully authoring essays this will have an impact on their readiness to tackle college-level work. Care must be taken when considering a learning disorder for your teens/young adults in that difficulties are not better accounted for by other conditions such as ADHD or anxiety. When these learning challenges go untreated in a young adult, they can significantly undermine self-efficacy and negatively affect their ability to meet responsibilities in the workplace.

Another neurodevelopmental disorder that could cause difficulties with learning is language disorder. Language disorder includes both expressive (the ability to produce vocal, gestural, or verbal signals) and receptive language, the process of receiving and comprehending language messages.

Substance Use/Addiction

Substance Use Disorders

Substance use disorders are significantly prevalent among young adults, especially in college. The 2023 National Survey on Drug Use and Health (NSDUH) found that 27.1% of young adults between the ages of 18 and 25 had qualified for substance use disorder in the past year.[2] For the purposes of this discussion, substances include legal (alcohol), prescription drugs (benzodiazepines), and illicit drugs such as opioids and stimulants.

According to the DSM-5-TR, substance use disorder is considered substance use that results in significant impairments in activities of daily living including academic, work, and social areas. The person needs to use more of the substance to get more of the desired effect and can also develop a tolerance for the substance. They also go to great lengths to use the substance or obtain the substance. Although experimenting with substances is often common among this age group, it is of clinical concern when experimenting turns into addiction and misuse.

Survey data found that the two most used substances are alcohol and marijuana. Roughly, 14% of those between 18 and 24-year-old meet criteria for alcohol use disorders.[2] College was once viewed as a protective factor that fostered resilience, built community, and provided resources that helped students develop self-efficacy skills. However, it is now sometimes associated with an increased risk of substance use disorders, partly due to social environments in which recreational substance use is more normalized. Although the social environment in college is a risk factor for substance abuse, national surveys have found that early alcohol and drug use before the age of 15 is strongly associated with developing substance use disorder later in life.[1,2] Specifically, a 40% increase in alcohol dependence was found for those who began drinking before the age of 14.[8] Other risk factors for substance use disorders in this age group are a history of childhood abuse, family history of substance abuse, individual risk factors (academic stressors, grief/loss), environmental risk factors, and co-occurring clinical disorders.[9] Teen and young adult substance use in social environments can also be a source of coping with stress and difficult emotions. When substances start to become a form of coping, avoidance difficulties can arise with attending to responsibilities. For this age group, substance use disorders would interfere with social, academic, and job obligations, preventing the full transition into independence as a young adult.

Technology Addiction

Internet web access has been available to the public since the early 1990s and the smartphone with internet access has been around for nearly 20 years. Since the advent of these forms of technology, mental health researchers began to recognize problematic clinical disorders and problems associated with excessive use. The current generation, commonly known as Gen Z, has been raised with this technology since childhood. However, not all young adults who have been raised with access to technology throughout their childhood will develop addiction to technology. Similar to risk factors associated with substance use disorder, the development of addiction to technology is associated with environmental, social, psychological, and familial risk factors.

The following are examples of technology addiction:[10]

A Social media addiction
B Internet gaming disorder
C Online gambling
D Online shopping addiction
E Problematic use of online pornography

Of this list, only gambling disorder is officially included in the DSM-5-TR. Internet gaming disorder is mentioned in the DSM-5-TR as a "condition for further study." The other technology addiction behaviors are not recognized as official clinical disorders although they cause significant impairments in functioning like the effects of substance use disorders. Adults who engage in addictive behaviors related to technology show the same signs as those who are addicted to substances. These signs include engaging in technological activities to the exclusion of other activities in their life (e.g., attending school and work obligations). They might find themselves using technology to avoid or manage mood and anxiety vs. using technology to either connect with others for fun. When young people who are addicted to technology use do not have access to that technology, they might experience withdrawal symptoms like those who are engaging in substance abuse. According to the World Health Organization, 11% of teens worldwide had problematic social media use and 12% were at risk of problematic gaming.[11] The impact of this addictive behavior is observed via difficulties in keeping up with obligations at school, work, and with friends. Addictive behaviors with the internet and other forms of technology have been seen to have a negative effect on brain functioning. Young adults who maintained an elevated level of engagement with digital use from adolescence showed decreases in short-term memory functioning.[12]

Autism Spectrum Disorder

An estimated 2.21% of adults in the United States have a diagnosis of autism spectrum disorder.[13] Autism spectrum disorder (ASD) is a chronic neurodevelopmental disorder with symptoms first observed in childhood. The DSM-5-TR categorizes ASD into three levels based on severity and the amount of support needed. These levels include the following: requiring support, requiring substantial support, and requiring very substantial support. Since ASD can be accompanied by intellectual and language impairments, for the purposes of how this clinical disorder can contribute to *failure to launch,* we will describe ASD symptoms in the presence of intellectual abilities within the *average range and above*. Young adults with ASD who are also diagnosed with intellectual disabilities naturally require a minimum substantial support from adult caregivers and would not be considered *failure to launch*.

Teens and adults diagnosed with ASD must demonstrate the following symptoms based on developmental history, current symptoms, and clinical observations:

1 Persistent deficits in social communication and social interaction across multiple situations specifically:
    - Difficulties in nonverbal communicative behaviors used for social interactions
    - Difficulties with social-emotional reciprocity
    - Difficulties in developing, maintaining and understanding relationships
2 Restricted, repetitive patterns of behavior, interests, or activities, as shown at least two of the following:
    - Repetitive motor movements or speech
    - Inflexibility regarding routines and patterns (verbal and nonverbal)
    - Hyper or hyposensitivity to sensory input or other sensory aspects of the environment

Teens and young adults in the ASD level of "requiring support" might be considered having high functioning autism. However, they may still experience difficulties with social communication and have unsuccessful attempts in engaging with others. Moreover, a level of inflexibility poses challenges with functioning in multiple contexts and switching between activities. They also experience difficulties with organization and planning. At this level, these symptoms interfere with effectively managing unexpected life problems, which hinders successfully transitioning to adulthood. These teens and young adults typically need extra behavioral support during transitional years to achieve and sustain independence.

Other Relevant Clinical Concerns

The following are behaviors or cognitive processes that do not meet criteria for a specific clinical diagnosis on their own but are recognized as clinical concerns that could increase the risk for *failure to launch* in young adults. Features of these clinical concerns can be often observed in the clinical disorders described in this chapter. Their lack of inclusion in the DSM-5-TR does not necessarily indicate that these conditions are less serious or problematic.

One clinical area of concern that might affect teens and young adults is deficits in communication. These deficits reduce the ability to be verbally expressive in an effective way. One such clinical concern that is not included in the DSM is auditory processing disorder (APD). This type of condition may overlap with language disorders included in the DSM and with ADHD. APD specifically focuses on difficulties with processing sound, as the brain has difficulty interpreting auditory information.[14] This condition is often diagnosed by audiologists. This condition causes difficulty with understanding speech in noisy environments, and difficulty following directions. Furthermore, APD can also result in difficulties related to learning, attention, memory, and language-related skills.

Another area of clinical concern that does not have a specific clinical disorder label is cognitive inflexibility/rigidity. Cognitive inflexibility/rigidity is commonly observed in clinical disorders including ADHD, autism spectrum disorder, depression, OCD, and personality disorders. This style of cognitive processing can lead to difficulties with problem solving, as it gets in the way of evaluating workable solutions and feasible outcomes. Furthermore, the inability to flexibly adapt your thoughts and behaviors when managing stressors can hinder behavioral success.[15] Cognitive inflexibility can cause significant distress and difficulties. Students who were found to be psychologically flexible reported greater self-efficacy, while those who exhibited inflexibility reported lower self-efficacy.[16]

As we have demonstrated above, clinical mental health disorders can have a negative effect on teens and young adults' sense of self-efficacy and developing appropriate skills for managing adulthood. Although this book mainly emphasizes *preventing failure to launch,* it is also important to consider clinical disorders that may heighten the risk of developing this condition.

References

1 Kessler RC, Berglund P, Demler O, Jin R, Merikangas KR, Walters EE. Lifetime prevalence and age-of-onset distributions of DSM-IV disorders in the National Comorbidity Survey Replication. *Arch Gen Psychiatry*. 2005;62(6):593–602.

2 Substance Abuse and Mental Health Services Administration. Key substance use and mental health indicators in the United States: results from the 2022 National Survey on Drug Use and Health. Rockville (MD): SAMHSA; 2023.

3 Terlizzi EP, Zablotsky B. Symptoms of anxiety and depression among adults: United States, 2019 and 2022. National Health Statistics Reports, No. 213, published November 7, 2024 (17 pages).

4 Danielson ML, Claussen AH, Bitsko RH, et al. ADHD prevalence among U.S. children and adolescents in 2022: diagnosis, severity, co-occurring disorders, and treatment. *J Clin Child Adolesc Psychol*. 2024 May 22;53:343–360.

5 Barkley RA. What is executive function? 7 deficits tied to ADHD. ADDitude. 2025 Nov 3. Available from: https://www.additudemag.com/7-executive-function-deficits-linked-to-adhd/
6 Larson K, Russ SA, Kahn RS, Kleinman A, Sclar DA, Olson LM. Patterns of comorbidity, functioning, and service use for US children with ADHD, 2007. *Pediatrics*. 2011;127(3):462–470.
7 Boat TF, Wu JT, Committee to Evaluate the Supplemental Security Income Disability Program for Children with Mental Disorders, et al. Prevalence of learning disabilities. Washington (DC): National Academies Press (US); 2015 Oct 28.
8 Grant BF, Dawson DA. Age of onset of drug use and its association with DSM-IV drug abuse and dependence. *J Subst Abuse*. 1998;10(2):163–173.
9 Alhammad M, Aljedani R, Alsaleh M, Atyia N, Alsmakh M, Alfaraj A, et al. Family, individual, and other risk factors contributing to risk of substance abuse in young adults: a narrative review. *Cureus*. 2022;14(12):e32316.
10 Sherer J, Levounis P. Technological addictions. *Psychiatr Clin North Am*. 2022;45(3):577–591.
11 Boniel-Nissim M, Marino C, Galeotti T, Blinka L, Ozoliņa K, Craig W, et al. *A focus on adolescent social media use and gaming in Europe, Central Asia and Canada: health behaviour in school-aged children international report from the 2021/2022 survey*. Vol. 6. Copenhagen: WHO Regional Office for Europe; 2024.
12 CDC. Estimated *n*umber of *a*dults *l*iving with Autism Spectrum Disorder in the United States, 2017. Autism Spectrum Disorder (ASD), Washington DC; 2025 April 15. Available from: https://archive.cdc.gov/www_cdc_gov/autism/publications/adults-living-with-autism-spectrum-disorder.html
13 Watson CS, Henrich CC, Long DM, Fobian AD. Longitudinal effects of adolescent digital media use on mental health in young adulthood. *Children*. 2026;13(2):215.
14 Drosos K, Papanicolaou A, Voniati L, Panayidou K, Thodi C. Auditory processing and speech-sound disorders. *Brain Sci*. 2024;14(3):291.
15 Frota L, de Souza P, Pellegrini L, Fineberg NA. Cognitive inflexibility, obsessive-compulsive symptoms and traits and poor post-pandemic adjustment. *Neurosci Appl*. 2024;3:1–14.
16 Jeffords JR, Bayly BL, Bumpus MF, Hill LG. Investigating the relationship between university students' psychological flexibility and college self-efficacy. *J Coll Stud Retent*. 2020;22(2):351–372.

13 When "Failure to Launch" Becomes Entrenched

The purpose of this book is the prevention of the *failure to launch*. We have spent nearly 20 years treating young adults with already existing launching concerns. Our treatment guide, *Life Prep*, was born out of our own professional frustration that clinicians did not have a guide to help younger patients learn skills to prevent this concern in the first place. Further, once this concern takes hold and gains strength, the treatment is longer term (usually minimally four to six months to years). Once a young adult becomes stuck (not launching), a multitude of concerns arise. At this stage, there are usually individual clinical concerns (e.g., depression, anxiety), executive functioning deficits (e.g., inattentiveness, poor organization), and support/system or family dynamics that are contributing to the major problem at hand. These variables need to be addressed with several interventions, some mentioned in this book already, but in a more time intensive and consistent approach.

Let us use a metaphor to illustrate why it is so important to use a preventative manual such as ours. If you were around someone with COVID-19 and you knew the possibility of contracting the illness was high, you would take preventative measures (e.g., wear a mask, ingest doses of Vitamin C, wash your hands with soap frequently, etc.). You take these proactive steps because you know if you do get sick, you cannot predict how your body will react; it could be as bad as a common cold or it could be life or death. Think of *failure to launch* similarly. Even if someone is a fantastic student, or responsible kid, you cannot still predict they will launch 100% successfully. Some are more at risk than others (e.g., those with a permissive family dynamic, or those with a history of anxiety and depression), but there is a baseline risk for everyone without these variables as well. This is why our program is for everyone and not only for those with a higher risk. Did the Center for Disease Control only recommend masks to high-risk populations (e.g., elderly) or to everyone? They made the recommendation to us all.

DOI: 10.4324/9781003649410-13

Evidence-Based Treatments

In this section, we will discuss two main evidence-based treatments for *failure to launch*. One effective treatment involves a multifaceted, evidence-based approach. This treatment requires participation from the young adult and the parent/support system. Cognitive-behavioral components are used, including cognitive restructuring (challenging unhelpful thinking), behavioral activation (engaging in pleasurable activities that require moving your body), gradual exposures (i.e., exposing someone in a gradual manner to more progressively anxiety-provoking situations, sensations, and thoughts), and executive functioning assessment/rehabilitation skills (e.g., organization, attention and their associated functioning/non-functioning systems). This model incorporates external involvement, including a functional assessment of how the family/support system may be contributing to the *failure to launch*, along with the application of parent management training strategies to differentially reinforce behaviors that support a successful transition to independence.[1–4]

Common deficits that often get overlooked and undertreated are executive functioning skills. This is why we have devoted the entirety of Chapter 7 (problem-solving skills), Chapter 8 (organizational skills), and Chapter 10 (goal-setting and follow through) to skill development that falls under the executive functioning umbrella. Acquiring and practicing these skills over time leads to a higher level of resilience and more independence as a young adult.[4] However, if left unaddressed, there are two steps we recommend taking. First, is getting a thorough cognitive assessment. This would have to be with either a psychologist trained in executive functioning tests, or an actual Neuropsychologist. They would provide you with a 8–15 page single-spaced report that details the functioning of your brain (e.g., how well you perform on standardized tests of sustained attention, processing speed, memory). Neuropsychological assessments are the most evidence-based assessment to determine if there is an actual executive functioning disorder (e.g., ADHD, dyslexia).[5] If there is, and because educational accommodations do not exist on the job, we recommend pursuing rehabilitative services. These can be with an occupational therapist, a psychologist (who can work on problem-solving, planning, goal setting and any interactions with anxiety and depression), and participating in remediation programs, such as Happy Neuron (https://www.happy-neuron.com/). Programs such as these are tailored for your individual needs and levels and then increase their variety and difficulty based on how you progress.

One of the newer evidence-based models for treatment of *failure to launch* is "SPACE-FTL."[6–8] Developed by Uri and Leibowitz, this model focuses more on assisting young adults through interventions with the parents/support system. It has five major components: psychoeducation, reducing parental accommodation, increasing parental support, de-escalation, and engaging supporters. Psychoeducation covers all that we have covered in our Chapters 1 and 2 concerning why *failure to launch* may have developed, what clinical factors may or may not be present, the role of behavioral reinforcement, family system dynamics, and executive functioning skills. In the first few weeks of treatment, parents/support systems identify how dependency is being maintained (e.g., financially, household chores, parents making appointments or encouraging avoidance). The next following weeks aim to reduce parental accommodation and increase parental support. The parents do not overwhelm the young adult, but focus on one to two impact behaviors that can be targeted (e.g., increasing involvement in household chores). The first few weeks lay out and cover, in a manageable way, the plan the parents expect the young adult (and themselves) to be held accountable. The intention of the next few weeks is for the transition of responsibilities to take place (from parent to young adult).

As sessions get underway (around week four to six), a high level of emotionality between the parents/social support system and the young adult can result in a breakdown or stalling out. Young adults can also become verbally or physically aggressive. Due to the high level of expressed emotionality that can result in the dynamics between parents and young adults in these situations, Lebowitz et al.[9] approached this work from the nonviolent resistance work (NVR) made famous by leaders such as Martin Luther King Jr. NVR is not a formal component of SPACE-FTL, but many clinicians use this model when they experience high-conflict situations.

NVR focuses on three main points. The first is parents/support systems focus on resistance rather than control. This means parents delivering their intent/message in a supportive and clear, non-defensive manner. Parents/support systems can perform "sit-ins" themselves where they express their desire for change in a peaceful manner. Parents/support systems do not retaliate when their young adult is verbally or physically aggressive but rather record it and help to keep all parties accountable.

The second component is called "anti-escalation" training. Parents are trained in the ways they contribute to escalating the emotional and behavioral components of a situation. For example, when their young adult gets angry at them for not buying them dinner, do they typically yell back at them? The model focuses on not responding to ways to reinforce the level of acrimony. Parents need to also be reminded that they have an equal part in the situation and for everyone to be on the same team, the young adult needs to feel things are being done for them, rather than against them. For example, your parents are not taking away your money for your gym membership, but rather giving you space and an opportunity to figure out how you want to maintain your physical health on your own.

The third component focuses on creating a larger support system/network. This support network is for both the parents/support givers and the young adult. They would be informed by the therapist as to the NVR approach (e.g., what would be helpful vs. not) and how to be a voice of consistency in the treatment approach and be emotionally available to all parties. Of note, this support system does not have to show up 100% of the time, but they are asked what effort they are willing to put forth in a consistent way. Could a sibling be an outlet for prosocial ways to cope with frustration?

Toward the latter sessions (week seven to eight/nine) in SPACE-FTL, it is recommended that the parents/support system maintain their expectations, schedule, and be consistent/predictable. However, this must be coupled with warmth and understanding. Parents must understand this treatment does not automatically result in a fully transitioned, independent young adult. What you are starting is the path to independence and over time, the young adult should engage in fewer avoidance behaviors, more independent problem-solving, increased responsibilities/self-guidance, and less pressure on the parents. It is not a realistic expectation that the young adult will have a job and be living on their own at the conclusion of treatment. However, it is realistic to expect they will have significant momentum in skills development that will eventually lead to that goal.

One of the measures SPACE-FTL recommends using to determine the severity of family accommodation in the launching process is the Family Accommodation Scale. It is available on the website: https://www.spacetreatment.net/fasa. This scale is available online and we highly recommend using it as a measure for baseline assessment, during and post-treatment. Other measures such as the Beck Anxiety Inventory[10] and the Beck Depression Inventories[11] can also help to assess the level of anxiety and depression a young adult may have prior to and during the launching period. These measures have good psychometric properties (e.g., high levels of validity and reliability) to be used to assess progress over time. In addition, the *Happy Neuron* program above, also allows for a clinician to track an individual's progress and to assign them harder tasks (structured like a video game) to rehabilitate deficits (e.g., short-term memory).

In our experience using both of these evidence-based models to treat *failure to launch* over the past 15 years, we have seen that treatment usually takes nine months on the lower end and two to four years on the higher, more typical end. It is more common to have someone come in for clinical treatment when the situation has become untenable and all parties involved are in frequent conflict with one another. The shorter the time it takes to get everyone on board with treatment, no longer resisting treatment recommendations, and working as a team toward the same goals, the quicker the treatment is a success. However, this treatment course usually tends to be full of stress and resistance for all parties involved, taking longer to resolve symptoms and gain meaningful traction.

Taking a Preventative Approach

The treatments outlined above can be demanding and stressful. Taking a proactive approach—by building skills, gaining relevant experience, and establishing a clear plan—can help you/your child avoid *failing to launch*. This path is typically more straightforward, more encouraging, and less burdensome than needing to engage in intensive clinical treatment later in life. The *Life Prep* program was born out of our own professional frustration with our patients not being equipped with the necessary skills to succeed as independent young adults by the time they needed to launch. After years of investigating schools, parents, and other clinicians, we discovered no one was providing these skills in a well-defined, structured plan. Thus, we reverse engineered our treatment work, including all the skills we found lacking across the board in our younger patients and developed the *Life Prep* program. Our program has been extremely successful in helping young adults launch; approximately 92% report having the skills to become successful, independent young adults. They reported that it not only accelerated their progress toward independence and goal attainment, but also strengthened their ability to handle stress, navigate conflict, and manage challenges along the way.

We want to provide you with our own quick assessment to help determine if your child may be in a position where there is an existing need for professional intervention (they should be at the age of launching-22/23 years old). Take our quiz below.

Please answer the following questions to the best of your ability.

1 Do you have a plan for your career/job after your formal education?
   A I know what I will pursue as a career/job and have a specific plan.
   B I have an idea of the career/job I want but have no plan now.
   C I have no idea what I will do after my education is done.
   D I have no desire or plan to do anything after my education.
2 What is your financial plan after your formal education is completed?
   A I have specific plan and have already acted on the plan.
   B I have a general plan, but no specifics yet.
   C I have no idea how I will be financially supported in the future.
   D I do not care about my financial concerns in the future. I believe they are someone else's responsibility.

3 What is your plan for a support system when you are around 22/23 years of age?
   A I have already reached out to my support system currently and have developed a plan.
   B I am pretty sure that I have the skills to be able to make friends wherever I am.
   C I know other people will reach out to me if they also value our relationship.
   D I do not really care, and it does not matter.
4 Are you struggling to leave the house you grew up in (22/23 years old/post education)?
   A No, I have already left, and I am living on my own (with or without roommates).
   B Yes, but I am saving up finances to be able to afford a place on my own.
   C Yes, I cannot seem to get a handle on my finances and save enough.
   D Yes, but it is the responsibility of my parents or others to help me with this.
5 Are you working in a job or internship? Or have you applied for jobs and received offers?
   A Yes, working in a job full-time or part-time.
   B Yes, working in an unpaid internship with the goal it will turn into a paid position.
   C No, I have applied to a lot of jobs but haven't received any offers after interviews.
   D No, I have not applied to any jobs and have no interest.
6 How are you feeling about your life after your formal education is finished?
   A Great. I have a lot to look forward to in my future.
   B Good. I have a lot to look forward to, but I am also stressed and scared.
   C OK. I think I know what I want to do, but I am still unsure and am having troublemaking decisions.
   D Horrible. I have no idea what I want to do and I feel completely lost.
7 Are you struggling with any anxiety, depression or a learning concern?
   A No, not a concern for me now.
   B Yes, but it is well managed with therapy and/or medication.
   C Yes. I am engaging in therapy but not sure it is helping.
   D Yes. I don't want any help. I can manage on my own.
8 We all experience struggles and hardships in our life. When you experience struggles, what statement below would best fit you?
   A I seek out support from trusted people in my life. I listen to input and decide what I put into action.

B I only listen to a few people. I like to think it through on my own first.
C I research what to do and decide on my own. Others' opinions do not impact me.
D I freeze. It does not feel good. I try to avoid it all.

If you/they are circling more "Cs" and "Ds" there is a moderately high-high risk of failing to launch or are already not launching successfully. If you/they acknowledge a wide variety of responses in each letter category ("A, B, C and Ds"), there is a moderate risk of failing to launch. Look at the questions you answered, particularly the "C's" and "D's," to assess specific severity. If it is more on the extreme or severe side and very prevalent in your life (happening most of the time), we recommend seeking out professional help (even if it is one question). If your responses are mostly "A's" and "B's," this book is your best option going forward. Responding with mostly "A's" does NOT put you in the all-clear. We work with plenty of patients who were highly functional earlier in life, had strong support networks and independent systems of accountability and they STILL failed to launch successfully. So, it is in your best interest to still actively and closely follow a preventative program.

If you do need to seek out professional treatment it is of the utmost importance you select a professional that is trained in this clinical issue. Many clinicians will say they do this type of treatment, but they do not. Ask your potential clinician the specifics above. You need to know that they are giving you the complete and comprehensive treatment that is supported by scientific research (evidence-based). Ask them about how they have approached cases in the past and the types of interventions they have used. If they do not know what you are speaking about (in referring to the above-mentioned actual treatment for failure to launch), you want to find someone who does and is competent. Websites we recommend are www.adaa.org or www.abct.org. Be wary of clinicians who overpromise.

References

1 Beck AT. Cognitive therapy and the emotional disorders. New York (NY): International Universities Press; 1976.
2 Foa EB, Kozak MJ. Emotional processing of fear: exposure to corrective information. Psychol Bull. 1986;99(1):20–35.
3 Kazdin AE. Parent management training: treatment for oppositional, aggressive, and antisocial behavior in children and adolescents. New York (NY): Oxford University Press; 2005.
4 Arnett JJ. Emerging adulthood: a theory of development from the late teens through the twenties. *Am Psychol.* 2000;55(5):469–480.
5 Medalia A, Freilich B. The neuropsychological educational approach to cognitive remediation (NEAR) model: practice principles and outcome studies. *Am J Psychiatr Rehabil.* 2008;11(2):123–143.

6 Berger U, Lebowitz ER. Parent training for dependent, yet abled young adults. *Bull Menninger Clin.* 2022;86(3):249–281.
7 Lebowitz ER. "Failure to launch": shaping intervention for highly dependent adult children. *J Am Acad Child Adolesc Psychiatry.* 2017;56(3):187–188.
8 Lebowitz ER, Omer H, Hermes H, Scahill L. Family accommodation in pediatric anxiety disorders. *Depress Anxiety.* 2013;30(1):47–54.
9 Lebowitz ER, Dolberger D, Nortov E, Omer H. Parent training in nonviolent resistance for adult entitled dependence. *Fam Process.* 2012;51(1):1–17.
10 Beck AT, Epstein N, Brown G, Steer RA. An inventory for measuring clinical anxiety: psychometric properties. *J Consult Clin Psychol.* 1988;56(6):893–897.
11 Beck AT, Steer RA, Brown GK. Manual *for the beck depression inventory*-II. San Antonio (TX): Psychological Corporation; 1996.

14 Conclusion

The Road Ahead

You may have read this book as a parent, a teen or as a 20-year-old. We are so proud that you are now knowledgeable about the skills to succeed as a young adult. We encourage you to re-read chapters and to bring in family members/support systems for discussion. Like parenting itself, there is no one way to launch correctly, but there are ways to do it wrong. We have discussed these ways in detail in our previous chapters.

When administering this program to schools we have frequently heard students say, "I already know these skills." This statement both amuses and confuses us because we ourselves have not mastered the skills in this book. These skills are always changing, developing, and are different for different people and stages of life. We need to have these skills to be able to apply them not only to the situations we can imagine, but more importantly, the ones we cannot.

When we are younger, especially later in high school, a lot of us can think we know all the answers, though some of us think we know none. Knowledge and experience are a spectrum. Just because you are president of an airline does not mean you know genetics. We all have limitations. It is having the awareness to recognize what you do not yet know, along with the ability to adjust your mindset and approach, that ultimately allows you to succeed.

As you finish this book, reach out to people in your trusted social circle. Make sure these people are not your competitors. You want to identify persons who have your best interest at heart. These can be a teacher, counselor, your own psychologist, older sibling, or anyone with whom you have a trusted relationship. Ask them about their successes in life and how they achieved them. More importantly, ask them about their failures and struggles. What went wrong? How did they make the wrong or right decision? Did they change their mind? Did they learn anything in the process? Learn from these trusted resources so you can avoid making their mistakes. However, expect that you will make plenty of your own mistakes along the way.

DOI: 10.4324/9781003649410-14

Recommended Sources

As clinicians, we have helped hundreds of people build successful, independent lives. Our clinical experiences have taught us there are many different paths to success and failure. This is why we want you to rely on our experience to guide you in the *Life-Prep* program. As the saying goes, "an ounce of prevention is worth a pound of cure."

In that regard, in addition to the Life-Prep program, we want to recommend sources we trust.

Individual Life-Prep Program online (taught by Dr. Kaplan) and clinician/school-based version
www.lifeprep.studio
Websites for anxiety and depression evidence-based treatment:
American for Behavioral and Cognitive Therapies:
www.abct.org
Anxiety and Depression Association of America:
www.adaa.org
Websites for Evidence-Based treatment for actual *Failure to Launch:*
SPACE (Supportive Parenting for Anxious Childhood Emotions):
www.spacetreatment.net

Conclusion

As we have covered, certain variables can lead us to be more vulnerable to developing *failure to launch* (e.g., being parented in a permissive style, history of executive functioning deficits, lack of accountability, etc.). Many *failure to launch* cases are from people we least expect; valedictorian, the school president, the star football player, or even the steady young adult who had always had a great head on their shoulders. Life is unpredictable and we now know everyone needs these preventative skills.

The *Life-Prep* program is meant for everyone from ages 13–30 and their parents/caretakers. The earlier in life you implement the program and practice its skills over different life experiences, the more prepared you will be to successfully launch. By its nature, life throws us curveballs and no one gets an easy ride. This book can give you the skills to be able to conquer the world and know that you can do it. By now, you should have a plethora of skills upon which you can lay the foundation for the rest of your life. We are as excited as you to see what you will do with it.

Index

For Product Safety Concerns and Information please contact our EU
representative GPSR@taylorandfrancis.com
Taylor & Francis Verlag GmbH, Kaufingerstraße 24, 80331 München, Germany

www.ingramcontent.com/pod-product-compliance
Lightning Source LLC
LaVergne TN
LVHW020831241026
850939LV00027B/396
* 9 7 8 1 0 4 1 0 9 3 0 4 6 *